"The Object Lessons series ach..... .. .......... .... to magic: the books take ordinary—even banal—objects and animate them with a rich history of invention, political struggle, science, and popular mythology. Filled with fascinating details and conveyed in sharp, accessible prose, the books make the everyday world come to life. Be warned: once you've read a few of these, you'll start walking around your house, picking up random objects, and musing aloud: 'I wonder what the story is behind this thing?'"

Steven Johnson, author of *Where Good Ideas Come From* and *How We Got to Now*

"In 1957 the French critic and semiotician Roland Barthes published *Mythologies*, a groundbreaking series of essays in which he analysed the popular culture of his day, from laundry detergent to the face of Greta Garbo, professional wrestling to the Citroën DS. This series of short books, Object Lessons, continues the tradition."

Melissa Harrison, *Financial Times*

"Though short, at roughly 25,000 words apiece, these books are anything but slight."

Marina Benjamin, *New Statesman*

"The joy of the series, of reading *Remote Control*, *Golf Ball*, *Driver's License*, *Drone*, *Silence*, *Glass*, *Refrigerator*, *Hotel*, and *Waste* (more titles are listed as forthcoming) in quick succession, lies in encountering the various turns through which each of their authors has been put by his or her object. As for Benjamin, so for the authors of the series, the object predominates, sits squarely center stage, directs the action. The object decides the genre, the chronology, and the limits of the study. Accordingly, the author has to take her cue from the *thing* she chose or that chose her. The result is a wonderfully uneven series of books, each one a *thing* unto itself."

Julian Yates, *Los Angeles Review of Books*

"The Object Lessons project, edited by game theory legend Ian Bogost and cultural studies academic Christopher Schaberg, commissions short essays and small, beautiful books about everyday objects from shipping containers to toast. *The Atlantic* hosts a collection of "mini object-lessons"... More substantive is Bloomsbury's collection of small, gorgeously designed books that delve into their subjects in much more depth."

Cory Doctorow, *Boing Boing*

# OBJECTLESSONS

A book series about the hidden lives of ordinary things.

*Series Editors:*

Ian Bogost and Christopher Schaberg

*Advisory Board:*

In association with

# BOOKS IN THE SERIES

*Remote Control* by Caetlin Benson-Allott

*Golf Ball* by Harry Brown

*Driver's License* by Meredith Castile

*Drone* by Adam Rothstein

*Silence* by John Biguenet

*Glass* by John Garrison

*Phone Booth* by Ariana Kelly

*Refrigerator* by Jonathan Rees

*Waste* by Brian Thill

*Hotel* by Joanna Walsh

*Hood* by Alison Kinney

*Dust* by Michael Marder

*Shipping Container* by Craig Martin

*Cigarette Lighter* by Jack Pendarvis

*Bookshelf* by Lydia Pyne

*Password* by Martin Paul Eve

*Questionnaire* by Evan Kindley

*Hair* by Scott Lowe

*Bread* by Scott Cutler Shershow

*Tree* by Matthew Battles

*Earth* by Jeffrey Jerome Cohen and Linda T. Elkins-Tanton

*Traffic* by Paul Josephson

*Egg* by Nicole Walker

*Sock* by Kim Adrian

*Eye Chart* by William Germano

*Whale Song* by Margret Grebowicz

*Tumor* by Anna Leahy

*Jet Lag* by Christopher J. Lee

*Shopping Mall* by Matthew Newton

*Personal Stereo* by Rebecca Tuhus-Dubrow

*Veil* by Rafia Zakaria

*Burger* by Carol J. Adams

*Luggage* by Susan Harlan

*Souvenir* by Rolf Potts

*Rust* by Jean-Michel Rabaté

*Doctor* by Andrew Bomback

*Fake* by Kati Stevens

*Blanket* by Kara Thompson

*High Heel* by Summer Brennan

*Pill* by Robert Bennett

*Potato* by Rebecca Earle

*Hashtag* by Elizabeth Losh (forthcoming)

*Train* by A. N. Devers (forthcoming)

*Fog* by Stephen Sparks (forthcoming)

*Wheelchair* by Christopher R Smit (forthcoming)

# hair

## SCOTT LOWE

BLOOMSBURY ACADEMIC
NEW YORK · LONDON · OXFORD · NEW DELHI · SYDNEY

BLOOMSBURY ACADEMIC
Bloomsbury Publishing Inc
1385 Broadway, New York, NY 10018, USA
50 Bedford Square, London, WC1B 3DP, UK

BLOOMSBURY, BLOOMSBURY ACADEMIC and the Diana logo are trademarks
of Bloomsbury Publishing Plc

First published 2016
Reprinted 2019

Library of Congress Cataloging-in-Publication Data
Names: Lowe, Scott, 1950 October 27- author.
Title: Hair / Scott Lowe.
Description: New York : Bloomsbury Academic, 2016. | Series: Object lessons |
Includes bibliographical references and index.
Identifiers: LCCN 2015043716 (print) | LCCN 2016013165 (ebook) | ISBN
9781628922868 (paperback) | ISBN 9781628922219 (epdf) | ISBN 9781628928570 (epub)
Subjects: LCSH: Hair–Social aspects. | Hairstyles–Social aspects. |
Hairdressing–Social aspects. | BISAC: SOCIAL SCIENCE / Anthropology /
Cultural. | LITERARY CRITICISM / Semiotics & Theory. | PHILOSOPHY /
Aesthetics. | DESIGN / Fashion.
Classification: LCC GT2290 .L68 2016 (print) | LCC GT2290 (ebook) | DDC391.5–dc23
LC record available at http://lccn.loc.gov/2015043716

ISBN: PB: 978-1-6289-2286-8
ePDF: 978-1-6289-2221-9
eBook: 978-1-6289-2857-0

Series: Object Lessons

Typeset by Deanta Global Publishing Services, Chennai, India
Printed and bound in Great Britain

To find out more about our authors and books visit www.bloomsbury.com
and sign up for our newsletters.

For Mary Beth—my enabler and muse

# CONTENTS

**1** Introduction 1

**2** Biology 17

**3** Removal 39

**4** Styling 69

**5** Fetishizing 111

**6** Conclusions 121

Notes 127

Index 133

# 1 INTRODUCTION

*Samson was the strongest man long ago*
*No one could a beat him, as we all know*
*And when he clash with a woman on top of the bed*
*She find out that the strength was in the hair of his head*
— **"Man Smart (Woman Smarter)," King Radio**

At first thought, a book on hair might seem silly. Who cares? Hair is just dead stuff, strands of keratin pushed out of our skin by glands and other weird gross things that are part of our bodies, or live in our skin, and make up the intricate colony of organisms that passes as a single human being, a person with distinctive attributes and a sense of individuality (which is largely an illusion). It's just hair, right? Why not write a book about epithelial cells, or the Islets of Langerhans, or the spleen?

Except that hair is different. It matters. It has an incredible power to annoy your antagonists, attract potential lovers, infuriate your neighbors, upset your parents, raise eyebrows at work, find compatible friends, and allow you to create, or recreate, your identity. While we think of it as a part of ourselves, it's also an object, one that can last for centuries in a locket or a grave, and cultures worldwide suspect that it might, at least under certain circumstances, hold your soul.

As a child, I first glimpsed the power of hair in Sunday school when we encountered the strange story of Samson and Delilah. As you probably remember, Samson, a judge and hero of the Israelites, received his superhuman strength from the uncut locks of his hair. Scholars have speculated at great length about the significance of Samson's unshorn tresses. The hair was the result of a vow made by his mother, not Samson, when God granted her a child. She raised her boy Samson from infancy as a Nazirite, or Hebrew ascetic, which is normally a voluntary, temporary state chosen by adults, not imposed on children, that requires avoiding all contact with the dead, eschewing all forms of grape products, and leaving the head and face unshaven for several years. After the end of the set period of ascetic holiness, the Nazir offers several animals for sacrifice and shaves his face and head, burning the hair in a sacrificial fire.

Samson, while called a Nazirite, does not follow the prescribed procedures. Rather than shaving off his hair in a ceremony ending his period of consecration, he lets his hair grow for decades, so that it forms seven locks. After much persuasion, and several deceptive answers, Samson eventually tells Delilah, his treacherous lover, that his uncut hair is the true source of his strength. She then has his locks cut off while he sleeps. Reduced to the strength of a normal man, Samson is easily captured by the Philistines, who gouge out his eyes, reduce him to servitude, and mock him in their halls. Over time, his hair regrows, his strength returning with it. The story ends with Samson pulling the Philistines' temple down on their heads, killing them and himself in the process.

What was it about his uncut hair that conferred awesome strength? How did a vow made by his mother, not Samson, give him superhuman power? Why did the Philistines, knowing the source of Samson's strength, allow his hair to regrow? As a child I found this story to be both incomprehensible and disturbing. I wondered if I could develop superpowers if I never cut my hair. Sadly it was impossible to know; men with long hair no longer existed in the 1950s. I had never seen one and assumed they were extinct and impossible, like woolly mammoths.

This is not to say, however, that everyone is equally baffled by this tale. For example, Raël (born Claude Vorilhon, in 1946), the prophet/founder of the Raëlian UFO religion, tells us that Samson's hair functioned as antennae for his brainwaves. When his head was shaved, the brainwave signals were truncated, leaving him weakened.[1]

Other male biblical characters are described as having gloriously long, pampered hair. In the case of Absalom, a son of King David, his hair seems linked with a narcissistic personality, a cause and consequence of his pride. It leads to Absalom's death in a way both edifying and ironic when his hair becomes entangled in the low-lying branches of an oak tree as he flees his father's troops after a failed insurrection.

Absolom's egotism, expressed in his long hair, leads directly to his death. Samson's wild hair clearly has a different meaning and far more power.

Women's hair gets less attention than men's in the Hebrew Bible; most of the rules concerning it appear in the New Testament. We cannot rely on ancient bas-reliefs or carvings to reach clear conclusions on the styles of women's hair in Old Testament days due to the Hebrew's aversion to representational art. The only surviving depictions come from the Israelites' enemies, who were not bound by the prohibition against graven images. In that art the captive Israelite women's hair is usually fully or partially covered, which suggests that Hebrew women in ancient times would not have appeared in public without some form of head covering.

Most of us in the West have at least passing familiarity with the many strange roles hair plays in Western religious history and cultural clashes; we tend to know less about other civilizations. All of them have long, complex, and complicated histories of hair styling, grooming, depilating, and manipulating, and each has its changing, subtle sets of meanings. It's a fascinating area of study, and one that tells us about ourselves as much as it sheds light on others.

In the last fifty years, we have seen the rise and fall of numerous hair fashions in North America, each conveying multiple emotional charges and meanings. My childhood, like everyone else's, was punctuated by hair traumas. Though the details of the suffering differ, nearly everyone can recount emotionally charged tales of terrible haircuts, ridiculous style choices (remember the 1980s!), schoolyard teasing, neighborhood bullying, and dramatic family conflicts—all that fuss over hair.

Throughout the late 1950s and the first half of the 1960s, my father insisted on cutting his boys' hair. He'd grown up poor in Key West, Florida, during the Great Depression, in what was then the most impoverished city in the United States. The US Navy offered him a way out, sending him to Duke for the duration of the Second World War and educating him as a physicist. Though he was now a white-collar worker scrambling up into the new postwar middle class, he wasn't about to squander hard-earned money to have his sons' hair cut, not for $1.25 *each*—that was outrageous, especially when he could do it himself. On the last Saturday night of every month, he'd haul out the high chair we'd used as toddlers, grab his Sears Roebuck electric hair clippers, attach the plastic guide that held the cutting blades a half-inch above the scalp, and begin his hunt for victims. My two brothers and I would split up, running frantically around the house, screaming in fear, at first feigned but increasingly real, hoping against hope to escape. As the eldest, I was often the last to be captured. Squirming and protesting, on a few memorable instances we were tied with rope to the chair, so that our father could complete his grisly task. (Try this today, and you'll be visited by Social Services!) Then for the next four weeks our mangled crew cuts would slowly grow out—uneven, ragged, with random cowlicks sticking straight up, large patches lying flat—only to be butchered again.

In the 1950s and early 1960s crew cuts weren't just normal—they were the rule. If your hair stood straight up, you might get a flattop—the crown of your head as level and smooth as a perfect suburban lawn—but under no circumstances was it permissible to grow hair longer than an inch or two.

When the members of the Beat subculture and the following, much larger hippie movement started growing ever-longer hair, mainstream society was outraged. The 1960s and 1970s were a time of great social conflict in the United States, with massive antiwar protests, a profusion of liberation movements, the sexual revolution, and the looming specter of widespread violence, possibly even armed insurrection. Battle lines were being drawn, and hairstyles, especially for men, provided instant identification of the combatants. In the multiple polarities of Us versus Them, all sides relied on hair to recognize friend and foe. It was a remarkably tribal time in a culture that thought itself to be modern.

Male hippies were hated for looking like women, which makes sense in the logic of gender distinctions—after all, everyone feels stupid asking, "Are you a boy, or are you a girl?"[2] Throughout the history of our species, rapid gender identification of strangers has been essential for survival (and potentially sex). While it is probable that there have always been gender-bending individuals within human societies, all cultures have created clear rules of dress and hairstyling to indicate gender and (usually) marital status. In general, we humans have a low tolerance for ambiguity.

Yet at the same time that the longhairs were accused of looking like girls, they were also taunted for looking like Jesus. Now *that* is bizarre. In most religions, the devout go to great lengths to look like the founder of their faith, even if their understanding of the founder's actual appearance is questionable. In the case of Jesus, scholars are confident that popular Christian imagery is simply wrong.

Jewish men in the time of Jesus had short hair. Jesus almost certainly did too. Even though Paul never met Jesus in the flesh, he knew many people who had. Paul was certain that his savior had short hair when he wrote, "Does not even nature itself teach you that if a man has long hair, it is a dishonor to him?"[3] So the longhaired Jesus of Western art is the product of faulty assumptions. Nonetheless, it is still widely believed that Jesus had long hair. The millions of drawn, painted, frescoed, carved, and sculpted images of Jesus created and revered over the last two millennia trump the scholarly facts.

Looking like our idealized, fantasy image of Jesus should be praiseworthy then—long hair, beard, sandals, and all—or would be if Christianity followed the patterns of other religions. For example, conservative Muslim men are expected to have long beards, with short hair and moustaches, because that was the style of the Prophet Muhammad. Shaivite sadhus grow tangled mats of hair in imitation of their dreadlocked deity Shiva. Buddhist monks and nuns shave their heads, because the Buddha hacked off all his hair when he embarked on his spiritual quest.

Imitating the hairstyle of your religion's founder is generally a good thing.

The negative reaction to the hippie imitation of Christ is quite anomalous then. It suggests that while it's fine for artists to depict the idealized Christ as an effeminate longhair, a teenager who looks like him is an affront to all that is good, decent, and holy. Such is the emotional irrationality of hair conventions!

In my hometown of Ann Arbor, Douglas Harvey, the infamous sheriff who terrorized Washtenaw County from 1964 to 1972, was noted for cutting the hair of every young male his deputies dragged into "Harvey's Hotel," no matter the charge. Unwary pot smokers, careless bicyclists— even hapless jaywalkers—all received buzz cuts for their transgressions. Everyone I knew loathed the man, but he deserves some credit for his intuitive understanding of psychology. He knew how to push our buttons. More importantly, the sheriff understood that men's hairstyles are intimately bound up with the social order. New hairstyles signify changing attitudes, and change threatens the already shaky social stability of the nation. Long hair was a declaration of cultural war, and Harvey—along with countless others in law enforcement worldwide—manned the trenches on the front lines of the generational battle of hair. The sheriff was more atavistic than he probably realized, since the punitive shaving of captured prisoners is one of the oldest methods known to humiliate the vanquished. It still works; as of 2015, hundreds of thousands of prisoners in the "rehabilitation centers" of the People's Republic of China are regularly subjected to involuntary head shaving.

Onetime presidential hopeful Mitt Romney's passionate relationship with hair was widely discussed during his campaign. In his days as a high-spirited Cranbrook School boy in the mid-1960s, Mitt was reportedly vigilant in identifying and disciplining those he judged deviant. In the most notorious of his "youthful high jinx," Mitt led his posse in an attack on a younger student who had incurred Mitt's wrath by sporting dyed blond hair, with bangs that fell down over one eye. While other boys in the gang held the terrified underclassman down, Mitt hacked off the offending hair with scissors. According to news accounts, the other boys in Mitt's clique remember the scene with remorse, shame, and horror, yet Mitt claims to have no recall whatsoever of the experience, a curious lapse in memory given that the attack was so primal and emotionally charged.[4]

A few years later at Stanford University, when Mitt and a small band of Young Republicans mounted a pro-war counter protest against a huge student antiwar rally, they displayed a sign offering free haircuts to their opposition.[5] It appears that Mitt, already a self-appointed junior commandant in the great American culture wars of the 1960s and 1970s, had become one of the hapless millions tangled up in the psychologically fraught net of hair.

It is somehow fitting that as a presidential candidate, Mitt's hair was on the receiving end of public ridicule. Perfectly coiffed and dyed Goth black, with broad swaths of white in the sideburns that evoked the Munsters for voters of a certain age, his hair was seen as a wholly artificial creation carefully designed to project a crafted, if inauthentic, image, both expression and symbol of his public persona and presidential campaign. Mitt, like all of us, has a complex relationship with hair.

When I started high school in 1966, long hair was just becoming common and still had the power to offend. My friends and I pushed the limits of school dress codes. The girls wore ever-shorter skirts; the boys grew out their hair. Occasionally someone would get sent home, but by 1968 the rules were relaxing too quickly for us to keep up. School officials were overwhelmed. After I left for college in 1968, I didn't cut my hair for five years.

By the middle of the 1970s, long hair on men had become the fashionable norm, especially among the truck-driving country music fans who had been the bane of the hippies just a few years earlier. Soon after long hair conquered Nashville, most hippies opted for a new look, with the exception of diehard classic rock musicians and countercultural idealists. Even now on a trip to the co-op you are likely to spot men with thinning white ponytails, a defiant symbol from their youth, like them now domesticated.

The so-called punks, who rebelled against both hippies and straight society, worked hard to offend as many people as possible with their hair and fashions, presenting a new front of defiance. The early adopters of garishly dyed Mohawks and spiked hairstyles, the taller the better, must have been gratified by the vehement outrage they provoked!

In this post-punk era, it often seems that anything goes. Hair, like piercings and tattoos, is more fashion statement than political or existential confrontation, but this is presumably just a temporary respite. It's only a matter of time before new hair wars flare up.

A number of scholars have attempted to find a universal code underlying the symbolic meaning of hair manipulation, a global theory of hair. This goal has proven elusive. It seems likely that while hair styling always has meaning, that meaning is not fixed or universal—it changes with time, place, and social group—and in secular settings it can mutate practically overnight.

What is most striking about hair symbolism is that while it is always potent and full of significance, any particular style or treatment will communicate a range of meanings—similar, radically variant, even directly opposing—in different cultures. Hair can be bound up with nearly anything that generates strong emotions, so hair's drama is continuously playing out in the realms of gender, sex, religion, and politics. It's hard to see how any consistent, unified theory of hair could ever be possible, when the meaning of different styles and modes of presentation varies so widely from culture to culture, and even within one culture or society. The most basic, simple actions, like shaving the head or covering the hair, have no fixed import. There is no obvious meaning linking the forcibly shaved head of a female Nazi collaborator in postwar France with the smooth scalps of Buddhist nuns or Sinead O'Connor. The Mennonite woman who won't go out without a bonnet and the young suburban mother who always wears a ball cap at the park are making very different statements, despite the generic similarities of their hair coverings.

No one can be a neutral noncombatant in the contested battlefield of hair. Every hairstyle means something, no matter the intentions of the wearer, but the meaning of hair is not determined solely by the individual; it is social as well as private. You may believe whatever you wish about the message projected by your or others' hair, but society will overrule your personal judgment with its collective view, and other individuals may contest society's consensus as well, imposing their own meanings. Even if you think your hair is meaningless, it still sends a message to every observer.

Several years ago, during a sabbatical, I stopped cutting my hair. I wasn't making a deliberate statement; I was just too busy to bother with it. Yet, I soon realized that my slovenliness was itself a powerful statement that altered my relationships with others. A cousin was infuriated; he insisted I cut my hair. My family made disparaging comments. Strangers avoided eye contact. When a panhandler on Duval Street in Key West gave me a sly smile of recognition, nodded, and offered me a cigarette, I realized that I needed to get a haircut—and start dressing better.

So, the way hair is dyed, shaped, managed, neglected, restrained, or set free always has meaning. Although the meaning will be clear to different observers, they may not agree among themselves on what that meaning is. Hair is vexing, and it is complex. Everyone has opinions about hair, so naturally the world's religious traditions have a great deal to say about it.

In Judaism, some forms of Christianity, and Islam, men and women are required to cover their hair when in the presence of divinity. A fantastic range of head coverings—burqas, shawls, yarmulkes, skull caps, the fez—can be seen at churches, synagogues, and masjid ("mosques") around the world, designed to meet this religious imperative. Yet elsewhere, as in the early European colonies of North America, *un*covering men's hair before God and secular authorities was an obligatory gesture of respect. This goes back to Paul in 1 Corinthians 11:7-12, where he claims that men hold authority over women, so women should cover their heads in recognition of their subservience. Men, in response, should take their hats off, at least when praying. In the Massachusetts Bay Colony several Quakers, whose faith required them to show respect to God but not to any mere human ruler, were hanged for their beliefs. Believing that they should bare their heads only before God, their obstinate refusal to take their hats off for the governor was a significant factor leading to their execution. In 1661, King Charles ordered the colonists to stop hanging Quakers; if he hadn't, the Puritans would surely have killed more.

The general topic of hair is huge, of course; the surface can barely be brushed in a small book. Therefore I have decided to narrow my focus to the religious meanings of hair. Why? Well, mostly because I've spent the last thirty years teaching religious studies, so religion is something I think about more than most topics, but also because religions care far more about hair than one might initially expect. Hair may be social or private, trendy or deliberately uncool, serious or ironic; hair is geographical, ethnic, and biological, but above all, I think it's religious. Of course, I think every topic can be approached from the angle of religion. So what might it mean to examine the specifically *religious* aspects of hair?

First, we need to ask what is meant when we refer to religion. The answer should be obvious and simple, except it isn't.

Religion is a multivalent word, meaning different things to different people. Though we usually assume that others share our general definitions of the words we use, once we go beyond pragmatic everyday vocabulary, this is rarely the case. Even scholars who have made the study of religion their life's work cannot always agree on the meaning of the term. For some, it refers to the doctrines and practices of the world's major faiths, the ones covered in introductory textbooks. For others religion and culture are broadly overlapping, nearly indistinguishable. We know that even a few hundred years ago many languages had no terms directly equivalent to our English word "religion." Yet every society on earth has distinctive attitudes, beliefs, and practices that address the fundamental human questions of meaning and purpose, life and death, sickness and health. All societies and cultures have religion.

For this book, we will understand religion in its broadest sense, largely overlapping with culture, as the sets of beliefs and practices that enable groups of people to find or make meaning in their lives, imbuing daily events with a sense of mystery, or transcendence, or simple comfort and security, in an uncertain, threatening world.

There are a large number of fascinating books about hair—both scholarly and popular—that approach the subject from other angles and different academic disciplines. There are even more articles than books, many extraordinarily perceptive, as I discovered while researching this project.

So why write yet another book on hair? Well, as I began investigating the topic, I realized that the profound links between hair and religion, while noted by nearly everyone, still haven't been addressed with the focus they deserve. Moreover, when talking with friends and colleagues, I realized that few if any were acquainted, even superficially, with the existing literature. The "truth" is out there, but spread among so many sources that it's essentially invisible. In this book we'll scan the world's hair rules, looking for meaning where it's evident. It will be impossible to cover everything, of course, but we'll try to hit some highlights.

Of course hair's symbolic power extends far beyond religion into politics, fashion, musical subcultures, ethnic identity groups, and broader social trends. And sometimes a hairstyle—even an outrageous or confrontational one— may have little symbolic substance at all, other than perhaps signaling, "I'm sexy," "I'm bored," "I've given up," "You can't see that bald spot," or a generic "Fuck you."

We'll start with a brief examination of the biology of hair, and then look at the practices and meanings of hair removal, hair covering, hair styling and coloring, hair fetishizing, and more, in a wide-ranging and necessarily spotty global overview. We will find that hair is unruly and rarely falls into neat categories. The hair regulations of every tradition contend with equal and opposite rules, sometimes in antagonistic religions but often within their own, making them challenging to categorize.

# 2 BIOLOGY

## What is hair?

One of the first things every elementary school student learns about hair is that it marks us as mammals, along with having warm blood, breathing air, giving live birth, and nursing our young. All mammals have hair, even dolphins, despite the fact that they look like they're made of slick gray rubber. Platypuses are not quite mammals, because they lay eggs and skip the live-birth part, but even they nurse their young with warm milk that oozes from primitive slit-like nipples, and they have hair, which aligns them with the mammalian camp. So hair is an essential identifier of who we are as mammals.

Hair and nails are the only parts of our bodies that regularly regrow after being cut off. Depending on the method, the location, and the remover's skill, the process of hair removal can be painless—unlike the severing of a finger, for example. Bodies will replace blood—if the loss isn't terminal—partially damaged livers will regrow, and our cells are continuously being renewed, but hair and nails are different. They regenerate completely, will grow to greater lengths than is biologically necessary, and they can survive on their own, without much visible change, long after being separated from a body. They are even believed to continue growing on the corpse after death. Though this is not in fact true, the belief is global. Hair and nail clippings are widely, maybe universally, believed to provide a powerful link to the person from whom they were cut; many cultures believe they contain the person's spiritual essence. The self-renewing quality of hair makes it especially suited for removal in coming-of-age rituals, mourning observances, and other dramatic intervals of transition, sorrow, and rebirth.

Hair is made of keratin, the protein-based polymers that form our fingernails and toenails, the same material that in other species is transformed into fur, antlers, horns, quills, scales, baleen, and shells, among other things. Our hair originates from roots deep within our skin, yet once it emerges its visible portion is dead, composed of relatively inert protein filaments. It's an object, not an organ or a living thing, though it is often perceived as being alive.

Many Rastafarians and Sikhs think that hair is a living organism, and commonsense observation supports them. Hair grows continuously and takes specific shapes—sometimes curly, sometimes wavy or straight, often on the same person—and for those of us with "difficult" hair, it's easy to believe that it has an independent will and personality. It certainly acts like an unruly living creature.

Hair grows all over the human body, wherever we have skin, with the exception of the soles of our feet, our palms, and our eyelids. We have, on average, around 1,000,000 follicles on our bodies, with about a tenth of them on our heads. Hair grows in places where most people desire it—head and face for men, heads for women—places where its aesthetic value is debatable—armpits, tops of toes, pubic regions—and places where some people wish it wouldn't—buttock clefts, women's chins, old men's ears, noses, and more.

Biologists have pointed out that humans have become increasingly neotenic over time, looking more and more like juveniles well into adulthood. The retention of juvenile characteristics—rounded features, "baby fat," relatively hairless bodies and faces—is believed to elicit natural caregiving instincts that are hardwired to varying degrees in most mammals. It's a clever evolutionary strategy to get the old to care for the young (and sometimes not so young!)

Neoteny works very well for dogs. When mature, even the scruffiest mutts are more puppy-like than adult wolves, and they inspire a great deal more affection. The cuter they are, the less work they are usually expected to do. If they're charming enough and have responsive owners, they can live royally pampered lives, just by looking immature.

Humans start to lose their care-eliciting features with the onset of puberty. Bodies lengthen, hair sprouts in awkward places—nowadays mostly hidden by clothes—features become more angular and coarse, as hormones reshape our bodies. Still it's thought that modern humans retain more juvenile features than our early ancestors. The hairy, beetle-browed, craggy, and stooped "caveman" is a classic cartoon cliché and a perfect illustration of what neoteny is not.

In modern humans, neoteny is especially noticeable in women. Not only are they generally less hairy than men, their bodies are more rounded, they retain strategic deposits of fat, their voices remain higher, more childlike, throughout their lives, and they generally have less brute strength than men. (However, they display greater endurance and in many ways are actually tougher than men.) Unlike other animal species—birds for example—female humans, in the Western world at least, are usually more colorful and better accessorized than males, though this generalization does not apply to all cultures and historical periods. In most societies they have created elaborate grooming practices designed to enhance their youthful appearance. Many of these involve hair.

Women tend to spend more time styling their head hair than men, though again this varies widely between cultures and historical periods, and women have been removing body hair for at least 5,000 years, perhaps because the absence of facial, armpit, leg, and pubic hair seems to evoke caregiving from males. We are trained to see relatively hairless bodies as "feminine," but they are also childlike. In recent years Western men have increasingly feigned neoteny through the removal of facial and body hair, shaving and waxing places that would have been unthinkable in the past. Male depilation has a much longer history in other parts of the world.

The Ainu, the indigenous people of Japan, created one of the few human cultures that seems to have bucked this trend.

After generations of assimilation with the Japanese majority, it is thought that no genetically pure Ainu now survive, but even the remnant genetically diluted populations are noted for their luxuriant hair. Ainu men have enviable beards, and until recent years Ainu women still sported moustache-like lip tattoos, despite the prohibitions imposed by the Japanese Imperial government. Perhaps it is not coincidental that the Ainu traditionally worshiped bears.

Human hair comes in various types: the terminal hair of our heads, bodies, and pubic regions; vellus hair, the colorless "peach fuzz" most visible on women and children, while often hidden on men below coarser terminal hair; and lanugo, the soft, downy hair that develops on fetuses in the womb and turns to vellus before birth. Curiously, lanugo hair often reappears as a visible fuzz on the faces and bodies of anorexics as they starve.

The typical human has between 100,000 and 150,000 hair follicles on her or his head, each of which follows its individual cycle of growth, dormancy, and eventual shedding. At any one time 90 percent of our head hairs are in a growth cycle, generally lasting for two to seven years, depending on personal genetic factors. If our follicles were to synchronize their cycles, as happens in some mammals, we would molt, shedding like bears in late spring. Instead we lose a percentage of our hair in every month of the year, throughout our lives. Given that the average head hair grows for about three years at perhaps half an inch per month, most humans cannot grow their hair much longer than 18 inches; however, terminal hair length, like other human traits, seems to fit nicely on a bell curve, with some humans displaying remarkably long hair and correspondingly exuberant, long-lived follicles.

Almost everyone approves of head hair. A full head of hair conveys an aura of health and youth. It's attractive, signaling vitality and, for males, virility, despite the fact that male baldness is often linked with higher testosterone levels and presumably stronger male sex drives. (Eunuchs rarely go bald; it's one of the unheralded benefits of castration.)

Yet while the presence of head hair is almost never viewed negatively, its absence often is. Conversely pubic hair is commonly seen as embarrassing or shameful and, along with the genitals it partially covers, is hidden by clothes in every modern society. Until recently, Western art avoided showing female pubic hair, or any body hair for that matter, in nude statuary and paintings. Male pubic hair, when depicted, was usually light and stylized. Even modern nudists, who claim to be celebrating the natural, unfettered human body, tend to trim or remove their pubic hair.

Pubic hair is much shorter than head hair, because it only grows for about six months before falling out. It's generally curly, constricted by oval-shaped pubic follicles as it emerges from the skin. (Many people have fairly round head-hair follicles and therefore produce straighter hair on their heads.) Asians' pubic hair is often fairly straight, presumably due to the shape of their follicles. It can also be relatively sparse.

Various systems have been worked out to classify human hair based on color, the density of the roots, the degree of curl, thickness of strands, and other readily measured qualities. The forensic uses of hair typologies in criminal investigations, common before recent developments in DNA technology, were often highly subjective and impressionistic, leading to fraudulent convictions as often as identifying true perpetrators.

We now know that the DNA in our hair contains traces of the entire evolutionary history of our species, as well as providing a means for identifying each of us that is even more reliable than our fingerprints. Our hair also contains a record of our exposure to chemicals—environmental pollutants, toxic metals, drugs—that can be read, somewhat like rings on a tree trunk, to construct a record of our past, enabling forensic scientists to trace our travels, measure our exposure to pollution, and assess our illicit recreational proclivities. Our intimate personal history can be reconstructed for as long as our hair endures. Long before anyone knew of DNA, people in cultures worldwide carefully disposed of their hair trimmings, sensing that the link between our dead hair and our living spirit could be manipulated by enemies for nefarious ends. Given the information that can now be derived from the analysis of our hair, perhaps we should be more cautious as well.

One of the most surprising discoveries coming from the study of DNA is the fact that our human ancestors, or at least those ancestors who migrated out of Africa, interbred with other, now-extinct early subspecies of hominids, an idea dismissed as absurd just a decade ago. For only a few hundred dollars, you can receive a precise readout of your own percentage of cave-person DNA. (I was delighted to discover that I'm 2.6 percent Neanderthal and 1.7 percent Denisovan!) Even if these initial results are corrected or superseded by further discoveries, they are still intriguing.

It appears that most of the DNA inherited from other early human subspecies has been lost over time, but select Neanderthal gene sequences have been retained, most likely because they confer valuable forms of disease resistance missing in the makeup of purer Homo sapiens sapiens from sub-Saharan Africa. More relevant to this book is the odd fact that a number of the Neanderthal genes identified in modern humans of European, Middle Eastern, and Asian ancestry are involved in the production of keratin, and therefore hair and nails.

The natural default color of human hair is black; other colors are due to mutations in the genes that determine hair color and texture. Light hair colors—shades from blond to red and strawberry—appear to be the result of a mutation similar to one found in the DNA of our extinct Neanderthal forbears, who we now know had reddish hair and light complexions. (The mutation that produces red and blond hair also produces pale skin color). At this time, there is disagreement about the source in modern humans of the gene sequences producing light hair and skin. Some believe the mutations were passed directly from Neanderthals to modern humans; others claim the mutations in modern humans arose independently. It has recently been suggested that the prevalence of red hair in northern Europe is linked to the lingering survival of Neanderthals there, assuming that they gave us the genes for light hair and skin. For what it's worth, red hair is tied to other fascinating traits, including high thresholds for sedation and analgesia.[1]

Hair color is often used to stereotype individuals in apparently arbitrary ways, though when examined historically surprising links can be discovered. For example, blonds not only have more fun, they're believed to be giddy, intellectually shallow, and perhaps sexually wanton. As we'll see, an ancient source of this modern stereotype may lie in Roman laws dating back at least 2,000 years.

# What purposes does hair serve?

Warmth? Given the generally sparse coverage body hair provides, it is close to useless for most modern people. The thermal inefficiency of human body hair is presumably one reason why clothes were invented early in our history, though some especially furry humans might have enough body hair to provide a bit of insulation from the elements.

Sun protection? Well, it's not as good as a solid pelt of fur but still excellent for shielding the head, and if it's long enough perhaps the shoulders, for those pale-skinned humans who must worry about sunburn. In Africa, where the need for sun protection is great, human hair is generally kinky and provides little or no shade for anything besides the head. Skin pigmentation has to suffice.

Does hair serve as a sexual attractant? Well, as Paul writes in 1 Corinthians, a woman's long hair "is her glory," which sounds like an acknowledgment of its sex appeal. The context suggests otherwise, however. Paul goes on to emphasize, "For her hair is given to her for a covering." He seems to think that hair can, or perhaps should, function to conceal women's features and preserve their modesty. As we will see, however, long, unbound female hair has been viewed as sexually alluring throughout human history, so dangerous that it must be cut or covered for modesty and self-protection. It serves as far more than a covering, a keratin headscarf.

It is often suggested that hair, especially in the genital and underarm areas, serves to enhance the retention of body odors and pheromones that serve as potent sexual attractants. The Mr. Spock in me rebels against the idea that our relationships with other humans are driven by subliminal sensory inputs, controlled by subtle odors and powerful pheromones we cannot consciously detect. Any notion so offensive to the logical mind is probably true.

We do know that in humans pubic and armpit hair is a primary indicator of sexual maturity, visually signaling our potential to procreate. The bodies of other primates are covered in fairly even coats of fur, with no noticeable genital or armpit tufts; mature female apes indicate sexual receptivity with the genital swellings and bright coloration of estrous. It seems significant that humans are the only apes that are sexually receptive throughout the year, and the only ones that visually signal sexual maturity with hair growth.

(Bonobos fool around daily but, like other nonhuman apes, only have full procreative sex when females are in estrous.)

Does—or should—hair serve to distinguish gender? Well, it certainly can, and in most cultures usually does, though facial features and hip-waist proportions may be more reliable indicators. Sometimes, as in the West, length is the revealing factor, but perhaps more commonly it is the way hair is covered or bound that distinguishes women from men. In many cultures, men have traditionally grown long hair, so the assumption that men's hair will be shorter than women's is far from universal. In the United States, men have been expected to have short hair since at least the time of the Civil War, when concerns for hygiene, uniformity, order, and unobstructed vision in battle became more important than the intimidating ferocity cultivated by wild, longhaired soldiers in earlier wars. By the dawn of the twentieth century, long hair on men was transgressive and shocking. At least one new American religious movement managed to employ the shock value of their transgressive hair and gender confusion to build a flourishing entertainment empire.

# Long hair, baseball, and the end of this world

In 1973 my brother and I stumbled upon the House of David, in Benton Harbor, Michigan. Founded in 1903, it was one of the most successful alternative religions of the early twentieth century, with hundreds of devout full-time members living communally on their extensive landholdings.

The House of David has a complex theological background that can be traced through several self-proclaimed prophets in the Christian Israelite tradition back to the millennial revelations of the English visionary Joanna Southcott (1750–1814). Its founder Benjamin Purnell (1861–1927) claimed to be the Messiah foretold by previous prophets. Within the community, his word was law, and he tolerated no dissent. He required his followers to be celibate vegetarians and allow their hair and beards to grow freely. While the teachings of the group are biblically based, they are decidedly outside the mainstream of twentieth-century Protestant Christianity.

As the community grew, its business enterprises flourished, and the group eventually became both prosperous and powerful. By the time we visited, however, the community was tottering on its last legs and appeared to be in steep decline. We saw no other visitors during our day there. The half-dozen members we met on the once-impressive grounds had been children when their parents joined the House of David and embraced the strict lifestyle and End Times theology the group espoused. Now their waist-length hair and long beards were turning white.

In the mid-1920s, just as the House of David was reaching its peak of prosperity, Michigan newspapers began reporting that Benjamin Purnell, known to his flock as "the Shiloh," "the Messiah," the "seventh messenger," and "revealer of the seventh seal," was secretly having sex with a large number of the young women and girls under his sway. This struck critical thinkers as duplicitous, because Purnell had long insisted that sex was antithetical to eternal life and would play no role in the "new Eden" he and his followers were creating. It certainly played no role in the lives of hundreds of his devout followers. The true believers within the faith dismissed the rumors (and ensuing lawsuits and criminal trials), but the community splintered and struggled after the death of its disgraced founder in 1927.

With sex forbidden and new conversions rare, the movement was ultimately doomed, of course, especially after Purnell's promises of eternal life for his flock were proven false; the Messiah's death from tuberculosis at the unremarkable age of sixty-six, followed by his disappointing failure to resurrect himself, made that clear. The old men and women we talked with were the last surviving remnants of this once powerful and creative community. At first, I thought they were too busy, or perhaps too cautious, to talk openly with their strange young visitors, but the men slowly warmed to us. It could be that they recognized us as fellow travelers, or at least sympathetic souls; we too were vegetarians, knew our way around the Bible, and had hair well down our backs. Whatever the reason, their wariness gave way to guarded acceptance. We spent a fine Indian summer afternoon, rapt in the fading light, as they reminisced about the past.

Being a child in the House of David in the 1920s had apparently been very exciting. Though the group's theology and lifestyle rules were strict, they owned dozens of farms and orchards, a wide range of manufacturing plants, a vegetarian restaurant, a beer garden, their own island in Lake Michigan, and most importantly, an extensive amusement park that was probably the finest entertainment complex the world had thus far seen. During their youth, these old men had had the run of the park, which was great fun, and they spoke fondly of summer adventures on High Island, the third largest island in the Beaver Island archipelago. When we visited, the decaying ruins of the park were still visible, as I recall, with miles of track for their eight half-scale passenger trains and the remains of a zoo and huge band shell.

Hair ran through all of our conversations. The men and women of the House of David had equally long and lustrous hair, and the men all grew full beards. The reason for their hair was never explained, as best I can remember—other than that it was a requirement of both the Bible and their messiah. My guess is that the Nazirite vow was involved.

In the early 1900s, the men's luxuriant hair had infuriated and alienated the local community in Benton Harbor, but it played a key role in the group's entertainment strategies. In their day, the House of David was known for the showmanship of their many theatrical and musical productions. They constantly invented new ways to engage and entertain their paying audiences.

We were told how the House of David's professional brass bands would go on annual tours, drawing huge crowds all across the United States. They would open their shows with their backs to the audience, long hair hanging down to their waists. At a prearranged dramatic moment, the whole band would spin about, facing their thrilled audience with their instruments and beards on full display. The crowds always went wild with astonishment and excitement. The musicians were men, not women! With long hair! And beards! It got a roar every night.

The thing is, of course, everyone already knew that the band members were male. People in the first decades of the twentieth century may not have had Twitter, but they could read. They had newspapers and magazines. The House of David was notorious everywhere their groups performed. Yet every night the crowds would be astonished and thrilled. The predictable, but still shocking, transgression of America's gender and hair correlations proved endlessly titillating back in those less jaded days.

The signals sent by the men of the House of David were curiously mixed, of course. The full beards projected masculinity and strength, at least to Victorians, while the long hair suggested effeminacy of the sort that was acceptable for Jesus, but not his modern-day followers. Certainly some of the power of their appearance lay in this confusion and intermingling of stereotypes and expectations.

The House of David's highly skilled touring baseball teams had their own angles for engaging crowds. The men, we were told, would stuff their hair up under their caps, so that they looked pretty much like regular ballplayers—only with beards. Then when they scored their first run against the home team, they'd throw their caps up into the air and their hair would cascade down, to the gasps, cheers, and scattered boos of the home crowd.

For several years they used an even edgier ploy: touring with a rival all-female team. The kicker was that the women were lesbians with their hair cropped into crew cuts. The publicity flyers trumpeted, "See the men with long hair play the women with short hair!" Probably the cleverest part is that the lesbians would openly cheat, spiking and elbowing the Israelite team and engaging in outrageous dirty tricks, with the calculated effect of turning the crowds' emotions from hostility to the House of David team to sympathetic support. It must have been great theater, especially since the House of David teams traveled with their own generators and lights, the first portable ball field lighting system in the world, or so we were told.

The House of David's teams weren't just transgressively longhaired, however; they were excellent! Usually playing at the Triple-A level, the top tier of the minor leagues, they would occasionally win exhibition games against major league clubs.

On an unrelated but intriguing note, we were told that the House of David created the world's first veggie burger. More significantly, they pioneered the use of enormous refrigeration plants to make fruit available year round, transforming the eating habits of the United States and eventually the world. Fruit would never again be only a seasonal treat.

Life in the community wasn't just about celibacy, sports, music, long hair, the End Times, and health food, however. The House of David is also credited with inventing the waffle cone, which they debuted at the 1904 World's Fair.[2]

*you should be women*
*and yet your beards forbid me to interpret*
*That you are so.*
—**SHAKESPEARE,** Macbeth, *Act 1 Scene 3*

It seems that in some circumstances people are more upset by women who appear male than by men who appear female, especially where facial hair—a purely male prerogative—is involved. Facial hair matters precisely because it is assumed to be an unambiguous indicator of gender. In the benighted past women with heavy beards often ended up in circus freak shows, so it is no wonder that some women have invested fortunes in time and money, apparently for as long as records have been kept, to remove unwanted facial hair.

At what point in our evolution as a sexually dimorphous species did women develop distinctively hairless faces? Did Neanderthal women pluck their moustaches? What about our Cro-Magnon forbears? You have to wonder when female facial depilation began. I would guess sometime in the Pleistocene.

There is a widely believed prophecy in Iranian Shi'ite Islam claiming that the End Times will begin when a bearded woman stands in the pulpit of the Great Mosque of Gowhardshad. The Twelfth Imam (a.k.a. the Mahdi) will then emerge from hiding—he's been living in reclusion, or "in occultation" as it is usually phrased, for more than 1,000 years—to lead the final battle against the forces of unbelief. More recently, a related rumor has been circulating claiming that, during a fainting spell, the late Grand Ayatollah Behjat (1915–2009) had a vision in which he saw the birth of the girl who is destined to kill the Twelfth Imam. It was revealed to him that when grown, this woman will wear a beard.[3]

Which is the greatest transgression—a woman preaching in the masjid? A woman with a beard? A woman who will murder the Mahdi? Fortunately, we don't have to choose; they're all linked in these prophetic revelations. Bearded women will do it all. Clearly, many Shi'ite Muslims see an obvious connection between "unnatural" facial hair, violation of gender roles, and rebellion against the divine order of the true religion. What better symbol for the overturning of true faith and a revolt against God than a woman with a beard?

# Hair versus fur

It's a common belief that humans have hair and animals have fur, and that there is some sort of fundamental difference between the two body coverings. There isn't. This hasn't stopped cultures from seeing their own members as elegantly coiffed and their enemies as fur-covered beasts.

In Chinese, as in English, hair and fur are different words. The Chinese word for their hair is *fa* 髮; the term *mao* 毛 denotes animal fur. In the nineteenth and early twentieth centuries, Westerners were known collectively as *hong mao gui* 紅毛鬼 "red-furred demons." It is thought that this term was coined in the aftermath of early Chinese encounters with Dutch seamen, some of whom had red hair and most of whom sported bushy beards. The Chinese have hair, of course, and usually grow only wispy beards, but Europeans have fur—not just on their heads, but all over their bodies! As we'll see, other ethnicities and outsider groups that violate the norms of Chinese culture—including ethnic Chinese rebels—are also described as having fur, not hair. Surprisingly, this includes the Japanese. Although they have relatively light body hair by European standards, the Chinese still called them furry.

On the colloquial level, we have all heard people refer to pubic hair as fur—do junior high school students still snicker every time they hear the word "beaver"?—but in my experience it is rare for anyone to refer to head hair as fur, except as a slur, unless perhaps it is extremely short and thick.

Freud believed that pubic hair fixations are the force underlying fur fetishes. The two kinds of fur—pubic and animal pelt—are psychologically entwined, so an excessive fondness for ermine or sable—especially with erotic undertones—can be understood as a displaced pubic fixation. Old mid-twentieth-century magazine advertisements for fur stoles certainly played up the sexiness of dead animal skins, showing cooing blondes caressing their new fashion accessories. If Freud's explanation were widely accepted, women might feel much less comfortable, or at least more self-conscious, about wearing mink.[4]

# Hair as difference

Hair holds the power to indicate allies and foes, potential sex partners and possible rivals, our group versus the others, to bond subgroups and alienate outsiders. American Indians were especially inventive with their hair styling; tribes could distinguish friend from foe at great distances. There was no need for colorful uniforms in the premodern world; armies could separate comrades from enemies by hairstyle alone.

Societies actively employ hair to manufacture the "Other," often by labeling the antagonists' hair as fur or by seeing it as primitive, savage, unruly, outlandish, or wild. The Victorian British reversed this common stereotype, however, arguing that the absence of heavy facial hair indicates weakness. As fanatical Victorian beard supremacist T. S. Gowing claimed in an eccentric 1854 lecture on facial hair, "The absence of Beard is usually a sign of physical and moral weakness; and in degenerate tribes wholly without . . . there is a conscious want of manly dignity."[5] The British used the thin and light character of East and Southeast Asian facial hair to argue for the innate moral and physical inferiority of the effeminate, weak Asians they had dominated. The smooth skin of the

East Asians was both a symptom and possibly a cause of their weaker cultures; the Chinese were essentially prepubescent or effeminate. From the Chinese perspective, of course, the heavily bearded, furry barbarians wore clear evidence of their subhuman bestiality on their faces and bodies.[6]

# 3 REMOVAL

**THE LAST NIGHT** (the final instructions of Mohamed Atta for the 9/11 hijackers)
1) Making an oath to die and renew your intentions. Shave excess hair from the body and wear cologne.[1]

In the aftermath of the September 11, 2001, terrorist attacks in the United States, the final instructions to the hijackers, written by their ringleader Mohamed Atta and recovered from his baggage, made quite a stir. Airlines were understandably panicked about possible new attacks, and security personnel carefully examined passengers for signs of recent beard removal. As I recall, several newspapers reported the case of two Sikh men who had their flight diverted and were briefly arrested, after they were discovered shaving their faces in the jet lavatory on an international flight. The irony in all this is that Mohamed Atta wasn't writing about facial hair—beards are highly desirable in Islam—but instead was telling his accomplices to remove their pubic and armpit hair in preparation for their translation into Paradise.

From the beginning of the Islamic faith in the seventh century CE, devout Muslims have understood that Allah takes a strong interest in human hygiene. His fastidious concern makes many demands upon those who submit to Him and follow the example of the authentic prophets He has sent. A famous *hadith* makes this clear:

> Narrated Abu Huraira:
> The Prophet said "Five things are in accordance with Al Fitra (i.e. the tradition of prophets): to be circumcised, to shave the pelvic region, to pull out the hair of the armpits, to cut short the moustaches, and to clip the nails."[2]

What is perhaps most fascinating about this quote, credibly attributed to the prophet Muhammad, is the claim that these five hygienic measures were practiced by the long tradition of Judeo-Christian-Islamic prophets and their followers, beginning with Abraham. Since we know that Muhammad received his revelations in a time and place where Jews, Christians, and pre-Islamic Arabs interacted on a daily basis, it seems likely that Muhammad's followers would know if this claim were false. We might infer then that these practices were followed by at least some Jews and Christians in the seventh century when Muhammad was alive. We know, of course, that circumcision was a requirement for Jewish males, and nail trimming was probably common everywhere. (A millennium earlier, in the fifth century BCE, nail clippers, along with a razor, were among the very few essential possessions the Buddha allowed his monks and nuns to own.) Short moustaches and long beards were common among Christians and Jews of the time, so that was a staple of regional religious fashion, but what about depilation? Did the Christians and Jews of the Arabian Peninsula pluck their armpits and shave their pubic hair? No one seems to be certain, but what we do know is that the Middle East was the ancient epicenter of body hair removal.

# In the beginning

The *Epic of Gilgamesh* is widely considered to be the oldest work of literature in the world. Growing out of even more ancient Sumerian poems, it seems probable that the complete *Epic* was first written in Akkadian. The later Babylonian retelling (ca. 1200 BCE) is the most complete version still extant. Fragments of the text exist in so many different recensions that it almost seems as if every literate Babylonian wrote his (or her?) own version. It was an incredibly popular story.

Gilgamesh is widely believed to have been an actual king, living around the twenty-sixth century BCE. By the time the *Epic* was recorded, he had become a semidivine hero, much larger than life. The people of his capital city Uruk were burdened by his demands and groaned under his oppression. They longed for a savior. The story is clearly more myth than history, though as an archetypical dictator Gilgamesh would feel at home in the modern world.

Early in the narrative, Gilgamesh, a tyrant and bully of unequaled strength, meets his match in a "wild man" named

Enkidu, who roams with the herds of grazing antelope, has never had sex, and is covered in fur. Gilgamesh sets out to civilize this feral man by commissioning a prostitute to seduce Enkidu and by hiring a barber to shave off all his body hair. It's an intriguing two-part domestication strategy, relying on unstated assumptions about what makes human beings civilized. Strangely, it works. Once shaved and sexually experienced, Enkidu is tamed and subsequently rejected by his wild animal companions. He now becomes a worthy partner for Gilgamesh's adventures. Already in the earliest work of world literature, body hair denotes wildness and savagery, while its removal (and loss of virginity!) brings civilization.

The Greek historian Herodotus, writing as an eyewitness in the fifth century BCE, reports that Egyptian priests shaved their heads, in contrast to the longhaired priests he had observed in other parts of the Mediterranean. He also tells us that the Egyptian priests stopped shaving and grew out their hair and beards when in mourning, again unlike the Greek priests who mourned by shaving, demonstrating to him that Egyptians provided a curious exception to the normal rules of civilized humanity.

Other authors report that full body shaving was normative for priests and nobles in Late Period Egypt (664–323 BCE). Affluent Egyptians of all genders removed all their head and body hair; priests additionally plucked their eyebrows and lashes. The wealthiest Egyptians hired full-time personal body shavers; if you examine the flint or copper razors used then—they come in many styles, with blades ranging from hatchet shaped to full circles—you'll conclude that only the highly skilled and steady-nerved would attempt to shave themselves. It was not a job for amateurs. Sugar and wax concoctions for hair removal, the ancestors of modern sugaring, were employed along with shaving to ensure thorough depilation. The wig business flourished.

It had not always been this way in Egypt. In the Old Kingdom (roughly 2686–2181 BCE) through the Middle Dynastic period (2055–1650 BCE), Pharaohs are depicted with real beards, often braided and powdered with gold dust. However, by the Late Period, Pharaohs, now fully depilated, are usually depicted wearing false beards, suitably dusted, as a nod to tradition.

Not only was this cleanliness pleasing to the gods, it is also possible that Egyptians found the extreme heat of summer more bearable without hair, though this is conjecture. We do know it made it easier to control the lice and fleas plaguing premodern human populations. (Biologists have determined that body lice evolved in close relationship with our species, so they were bugging our ancestors long before the dawn of history. In fact human pubic lice, which are distinct from human head lice, appear to have diverged from gorilla lice roughly three million years ago, so they've been hanging out in pubic hair since the time when our ancestors first spread across the savannah.[3] This suggests that our ancestors have had distinct pubic tufts for at least three million years.)

# Shaving, covering, and the global hair trade

Orthodox Jewish women have a long history of covering, cropping, or even shaving their head hair, beginning at the time of marriage. Though not obviously based on biblical injunctions—beyond the exhortations to humility and modesty in the Torah—these practices carry the weight of religious law. While the initial motive seems to have been to make married women, viewed as property, less attractive to potential adulterous sex partners, modern women now often wear extremely fashionable wigs, made from human hair, that arguably look better than their actual hair would if left intact. Attractive wigs are now the norm, so the original intent of the practice may have been lost.

Claire Accuhair, an upscale Brooklyn-based emporium, produces wigs targeted primarily at orthodox and ultra-orthodox Jewish women. These wigs can easily cost $4,000, plus another $600 or so for a high-quality shampoo, cut, and styling—it makes good sense to pay for an outstanding cut, because mistakes won't grow out. Claire Accuhair's website advertises its wigs with the slogan, "The Rolls Royce of Human Hair Wigs—Since 1960" and proclaims that its wigs are made from "100% unprocessed virgin European hair."[4] This is a bit surprising, because South and East Asian hair is considered by many to be the most desirable wig material in the world, as it tends to be long, thick, straight, lustrous, and readily available.

The source of much of the human hair used in wigs worldwide is India, though serious competition is coming from China, Mongolia, and recently South America. The trade in Indian hair is an outgrowth of long established religious practices of sacrifice, in which female devotees on pilgrimage shave their head hair and present it as an offering to a deity.

Tirupati Balaji Temple in Andhra Pradesh, dedicated to the god Venkateshwara, a South Indian form of Vishnu, is perhaps the single largest source of human wig hair in the world. Not coincidentally, this temple is also commonly believed to be India's wealthiest. The actual deity to whom the hair is offered at the temple is not Venkateshwara, but his female consort, known locally as Neela Devi. Over a ton of hair is collected on a typical day, which temple workers bind up to be sold at auction.[5] These huge mounds of hair bring a great deal of money to the temple; up until recently the majority of it ended up in wigs for orthodox Jewish women. However, in the last decade or so, as rabbinic authorities have learned that the hair coming from India has been consecrated to "idols," they have moved against its use. Neela Devi might not be Baal or Moloch, the heathen gods against whom the ancient prophets railed, and wearing a wig made from Indian hair surely isn't as offensive to YHWH as, say, eating pork from the altar of Zeus, but it's always advisable to avoid angering the Almighty.

For several decades, very different traditions of female head shaving in two widely separated religions created an improbable economic relationship, in which Hindu women sacrificed their hair to their gods, and Jewish women wore that hair in place of their own. International trade networks made this exchange possible, and the global exchange of information ended it. We needn't worry about temple income, however. Indian hair is still in high demand for extensions, wigs, and weaves; the African-American hair industry sees to that.

Wig makers catering to orthodox Jewish women have been forced to find other sources. Eastern European hair was once readily available, but with rising affluence in the former Soviet bloc, it has become increasingly expensive and difficult to procure. Nowadays most of the "European" hair used in wigs comes from South America, cut from the heads of the descendants of European immigrants, occasionally at gunpoint by organized gangs of hair bandits, according to the BBC.[6] While it is technically hair of European derivation, most of the "European" hair in North American wigs comes from the southern hemisphere.

# Islam now

Modern Muslim men continue to practice a limited form of body depilation, removing only armpit and pubic hair. Torso, arm, and leg hair is usually left undisturbed. Head hair is neatly trimmed and kept short, beards are also trimmed but usually long.

In westernized urban areas, men now often take a casual attitude toward ritual hair removal. However, anecdotal evidence suggests that even secular, nonpracticing Muslim men often remove at least their armpit hair. A few years ago, a Turkish atheist acquaintance expressed astonishment when he discovered that American men don't shave their armpits. He assumed all men on earth removed disgusting armpit hair; every male he knew did. As far as I could tell, he had no idea that the custom had anything to do with religion or was an Islamic mandate.

Even, or especially, tough guys like the Taliban of Afghanistan insist on following what they believe to be a fundamental religious requirement. As Christian Bromberg notes:

> When the Taliban came to power in Kabul in 1996, one the first measures they took was to impose strict hairstyle standards by force. Beards were to be large enough to be held by all five fingers, hair on the head could not be too long, and armpits and pubis were to be hairless. Radio Shariah (Islamic Law Radio) occasionally reported that individuals had been whipped, even imprisoned, for failing to respect such principles.[7]

You've got to marvel at fanatical religious conservatives who flagellate men for *not* shaving their armpit and pubic hair. (I'm curious to know who checks!) Dr. Freud would undoubtedly have had a great deal to say about this, and it certainly reinforces the point that all hair rules are bound by time, place, religion, and culture.

Hamam, Turkish-style bathhouses, segregated by gender, provide a convivial gathering place for women, where hair removal is an essential part of the beautification and relaxation process. Though shaving might seem an option, Muslim women rarely use it. Plucking, waxing, sugaring, threading, and chemical depilation are all preferred, perhaps because they last longer. Enquiring minds naturally want to know how often body hair is removed. The answer, I've been told, is that hair can be allowed to grow until it reaches the length of a grain of rice. The kind of rice isn't specified, so this is a pretty general rule of thumb, but presumably it shouldn't get much longer than a third of an inch, before it is removed.

Young Muslim girls and unmarried women are expected to retain their body hair until right before marriage, when the whole body is depilated, from the neck down, and the eyebrows are shaped. As a result teenagers are hairy, while married women revert to the smoothness of childhood. This creates the fascinating life-stage pattern of smooth children, hairy teenagers, and smooth, seemingly infantile adults. It's tempting to see Muslim depilation as a continuation of the ancient customs of pharaonic Egypt, but, while plausible, the evidence for a direct link is weak.

Through a marvelous convergence of customs, total pubic hair removal is now quite fashionable in the West, though some claim the fad is waning. The name given to the style of complete depilation—the Sphinx—presumably refers to the homophonous Sphynx breed of hairless cat, but it might just as well harken back to ancient Egyptian practices. Many observers have suggested this depilatory trend is a consequence of the mainstreaming of pornography.

Adult film actors have been trimming pubic hair since the 1980s and have been removing it all since the 1990s, providing greater visual access for the voyeuristic lens. In this case, a venerable religious practice required of Muslims, based on Allah's injunctions for cleanliness and modesty, ends up being independently adopted by adult film actors and their fans for erotic visibility. Pious Muslim grandmothers and fashionable women in the West are now equally hairless, as are Taliban soldiers and male "adult" performers in Van Nuys. In this case, religious fundamentalism and porn-star chic lead to the same place!

Some Hindu women, and even some men, are also reported to remove body hair, though this seems to be far less common than in Islam. Other Hindus make a point of deliberately not removing their hair to distinguish themselves from Muslims. In online forums Hindu trolls make fun of Muslims for their depilation practices, while Muslims taunt Hindus for their gross hairiness.

# Removal techniques

Ancient hair removal technologies are ingenious, though not necessarily safe. Chemical depilation seems especially questionable, using highly caustic ingredients, many of which are dangerous on their own and presumably even more toxic in combination. In Iran, it was and is common to remove pubic hair with a depilatory compound called *vajibt*, which contains yellow arsenic, active lime, and wood ash.[8] Depilatory creams made with arsenic have proven so popular in Iran over the course of centuries that the rinse water from hair removal has percolated into the ground table, adding significant contamination to the drinking water.

Scholars of Renaissance art have suggested that some European women also removed their pubic hair. You would think we would have copious written sources for this if it were the custom, but that's not the case. We do have recipes for depilatory creams, however, recorded in books of "secrets" written for Renaissance literati. Where they were used was left to their readers' discretion.

It seems likely that cultural borrowing from the Middle East, transmitted by returning Crusaders, was behind the depilatory creams employed by European women during the Renaissance, since the formulas make liberal use of arsenic and lime. A recipe from a book published in 1532 prescribes removing hair by boiling a "pint of arsenic and eighth of a pint of quicklime," then applying the paste to the target area. When the burning sensation feels intense, one is to wash the goo off quickly so the skin isn't removed along with the hair![9] Evidence for similar depilatory creams goes back as far as 5,000 years in the Middle East, so it's certain they are effective; however, this is something you definitely don't want to try at home. There are potentially safer recipes, as well, including one made from cat feces dissolved in vinegar, but you have to wonder if (and how!) it works.

Sugaring, the use of sticky sugar syrups to pull out hair, is remarkably effective, and is used extensively to remove unwanted facial hair, as is threading, the rolling of strands of string rapidly across the skin. Both methods catch hair and pull it out by the roots, in ways that are quick but painful.[10] It is often claimed that with regular use, these methods become less traumatic. Evidently the hair roots realize that resistance is futile and put up less fight.

# Hair, sexuality, and identity

Anthropologists and others have extensively discussed the connection between hair—styling, cutting, and shaving—and sexuality. E. R. Leach's "Magical Hair" is a notable example from 1958. In that article, he surveys a number of theories about the libidinal implications of hair manipulation, including the claim advanced by psychoanalysts that the head is symbolic of the penis and hair represents semen. Following from this it is claimed that head shaving is near-universally viewed as symbolic castration and functions as a means to control aggressive impulses.[11] Many critics have pointed out that even if this symbolic reading is accurate, it only applies to men, leaving women completely out of the picture.

However, the supposed link between head shaving and castration is not necessarily as silly as it sounds, despite the strong counterevidence provided by the millions of powerful men all over the globe who now shave their heads. Some ethnographic evidence seems to provide partial support for the assertion. For example, many Buddhist monks and nuns appear curiously sexless, their shaven heads (and in Thailand shaven eyebrows) making gender identification difficult. This is exactly the point, of course. Celibate monks and nuns renounce their mammalian status—mammals being distinguished by sexual reproduction, live birth, nursing of their young, and hair—so hair removal signals separation from the world of flesh, bodies, sex, and reproduction. It pretty much works, for both monks and nuns, even if castration isn't exactly what it signifies.

I discovered this to my embarrassment at a conference in Thailand a decade ago, when I sat down to eat lunch next to a Buddhist monk only to discover a few hours later that the soft-featured "monk" I'd been chatting with was, in fact, Thailand's first modern Theravada nun. While a definite faux pas—nuns aren't supposed to sit with men, so men obviously shouldn't seat themselves next to them—the mistake was understandable, or so I tell myself. I wasn't expecting to see a nun, because the Thai line of bhikkhunis (fully ordained Theravada nuns) died out centuries ago, as most books on Buddhism will tell you. The first nun in modern times, Dhammananda Bhikkhuni, the former professor Dr. Chatsumarn Kabilsingh, was ordained only in 2003.

As luck would have it, she was the conference presenter I had chosen to sit by at lunch. So I have the excuse that I wasn't expecting to see a nun, the odds against it being enormous, but the real issue is that I simply didn't recognize her as a woman. In retrospect, she didn't look like a man either, but that's just the point. Head shaving can make one genderless, much like the hairless, big-eyed aliens who abduct so many of our fellow Americans.

It doesn't work that way for Bruce Willis, however.

Buddhism traditionally views hair, like the rest of the body, as revolting. Elaborate meditations have been developed to create aversion to the body and its potential allure. (Advanced Buddhist meditators are supposed to transcend all craving and repulsion, so this cultivation of disgust is only a temporary expedient to help beginning and intermediate meditators conquer sexual attraction.) In all, thirty-two body parts are selected for analysis and contemplation. Buddhaghosa, a renowned fifth century South Indian Buddhist scholar, wrote the classic Theravada text *The Path of Purification,* which gives us a complete list. Vile item number one? Hair. We immediately learn that "head hairs are repulsive in colour as well as in shape, odour, habitat, and location."[12]

Things don't get better, as we soon read, "But just as pot herbs that grow on village sewage in a filthy place are disgusting to civilized people and unusable, so also head hairs are disgusting since they grow on the sewage of pus, blood, urine, dung, bile, phlegm, and the like."[13] Buddhaghosa classifies body and head hair as different entities, viewing them as distinct in nature, but both are revolting, of course.

In orthodox Buddhism, hair, viewed as alluring and sexually appealing by ordinary laypersons, is transformed into something disgusting and repulsive. The descriptions in classical texts are excessively graphic, perhaps because the authors realize that making the human body appear repugnant is a hard sell, at least when your primary audience is young, celibate, sexually frustrated novices. Young monks and nuns obviously understand the *idea* that the human body is gross, but grasping it on a thoroughgoing somatic level is the challenge. Humans seem to be hardwired for sexual attraction, and good hair is a big part of the appeal.

Head shaving removes one of our most potent sources of vanity and attractiveness, conferring spiritually desirable anonymity upon religious renunciates. It also removes a good deal of temptation, by making the shaven-headed monks and nuns significantly less attractive to potential seducers (including each other).

In medieval China crafty criminal fugitives realized that if they shaved their heads and put on monks' robes they could blend into the crowds in big cities, becoming indistinguishable from the many legitimate religious mendicants begging on the streets. Head shaving is not only spiritually humbling, it also erases one of the most crucial identifying features of any individual and makes eyewitness verification much more difficult. With a newly assumed Buddhist identity, it was easy to avoid recognition and arrest.

The Buddhist establishment eventually realized it would have to go further to distinguish its authentic monks and nuns from criminal impostors. Shaven heads were not sufficient. Their solution was to add scarification to the ordination ceremonies. During ordination rows of incense cones would be affixed to the freshly shaven pates of new monks and nuns and then lit. As the ceremony progressed the incense would burn down into the scalp, guttering out against the skull. After healing, the heads of legitimate monks and nuns featured rows of raised scars, each looking like the cone of a tiny volcano, marking them for life. Few criminals had the foresight or fortitude to endure the pain of these burns on the off chance they would need a Buddhist disguise sometime in the future. While the People's Republic of China has discouraged this practice, you can still see the old scars on the heads of monks and nuns ordained in Taiwan, Hong Kong, and other parts of the Chinese diaspora

## Meanwhile in India . . .

Some Hindu ascetics also shave their heads regularly, while others grow long matted locks (*jata*). Many scholars have noted that even though allowing hair to grow into neglected mats seems diametrically opposed to cleanly shaving the head, both forms of asceticism symbolize the same thing—the rejection of sexuality. However, the implications of the two hair strategies are not identical.[14] In India religious head shaving is associated with complete denial of sexuality and the practice of "respectable," orderly religious life. Monks in the tradition of Adi Shankara (ca. 800 CE), one of the great teachers of Advaita Vedanta, usually have shaven heads, at least during periods of their monastic careers, and are noted for their sexual restraint and morally proper behavior. When they allow their hair to grow longer, they keep it well groomed.

Ascetics with matted locks are far less reliable. They tend to be untamed, wild, and often violate the norms of orderly religion. Most are worshipers of Shiva or The Goddess, Shiva's consort. Many of them smoke ganja. Dreadlocked ascetics are often rigorously celibate, as is their tutelary deity Shiva, but their sexual restraint is not due to concern with morality. It is for gaining power.

Ancient Hindu tales of rishis, sages, and yogis frequently extol extreme acts of asceticism. Unlike Christian asceticism, which often seems driven by a sense of unworthiness, guilt, or sin, Indian asceticism (*tapas*) is self-inflicted torture designed to please a god or goddess who will then reward the ascetic with boons of wealth, long life, material fulfillment, or spiritual powers—powers which can be employed for good or ill. Many of the *asanas*, or poses, that are now taught in modern yoga classes were originally devised as forms of ascetic practice, because they were difficult and painful. They were not envisioned as part of a system of calisthenics, and they were not created to tone muscles, soothe stressed-out professional people, and mold healthy, flexible, sexy bodies.

They were created and employed to gain power. Celibacy is part of this process. Ejaculation squanders energy, and stored energy is power. Celibacy makes the ascetics' dreads especially potent, filled with *shakti* (divine energy). Dreadlocked ascetics may, in fact, avoid ejaculation, but this does not mean that they are necessarily well behaved, reliable, or "safe" in a pious religious sense. Their celibacy, torturous yoga poses, and matted dreadlocks are all part of the process of gaining power, and, as we all know, the pursuit of power and the search for holiness are very different things.

Buddhist and Hindu depilation methods seem quite moderate when compared with the Jain practice. The Jains firmly enter history in the fifth century BCE, roughly the same time as Buddhism, with the advent of Mahavira ("Great Hero"), the title given to the man who is often cited as "the founder" of the faith. According to the Jains' own accounts, Mahavira was a restorer of the faith, not the founder of their religion. In their view he is the twenty-fourth and last Tirthankara ("Ford Finder") of this world cycle, who took human birth to revive the forgotten knowledge of the path across the river of suffering to liberation on the farther shore. The Jains assert that their religion is unfathomably ancient, and based on their remarkably austere beliefs and practices, it's easy to believe them.

There are two major orders of Jain monastics. The monks of the Digambara ("Sky clad," or naked) sect are, as their name suggests, noted for never wearing clothes. This is still edgy in India, even after millennia of religious nudity.

Digambara nuns, however, wear simple white robes for safety, modesty, and as a concession to public standards of decency. Because of this, it is widely believed that they cannot become liberated. Owning as much as a single robe (or bowl or cup or toothbrush or razor or scissors or sandals) presents an insurmountable barrier to liberation, so the only option for Digambara women is to earn merit in this life with the hope of being born in a male body in the future. Lay Digambara males cannot be liberated either, because they own things. The sect is not so much sexist as "possessionist." This is a faith that offers the possibility of liberation only for a few naked homeless men who are very serious about self-denial.

The Shvetambara sect of Jains allows both monks and nuns to own a set of robes, because they believe that nudity is not a requirement for liberation. Though it is tempting to think of the Shvetambaras as a less rigorous group, in fact, they're just more pragmatic. All Jains are extraordinarily severe in their asceticism, as suggested by the fact that both major sects teach that the most karmically beneficial death, at least for those who are spiritually mature, comes from self-imposed, voluntary starvation. You should wait until you're decrepit and nearing the end of life before attempting this. Mahavira held off until he was seventy-two. According to Jain legends, Mahavira's emaciated body dissolved into thin air, leaving behind only hair and nails.

As you might expect in a religion that holds such a dim view of luxury items like clothes and bowls, the Jains take a hard line on head and facial hair. Shaving would be too easy (and might require owning a razor), so they pull their hair out by hand. Most monks and nuns do this twice a year. Jains believe that self-imposed suffering burns off past karma, so there are multiple benefits to this practice. It is now increasingly common for lay Jains—who do not expect to become liberated in this life—to pull their head hair out as a penance.

I once attended the screening of a documentary, made by a female scholar, of a Jain monk tearing out his hair. There were no special effects and no cuts, just real-time, hands-on footage. The movie began by showing the monk, with several inches of hair growth covering his head and face, grabbing a small handful of beard on the side of his head and giving it a tremendous jerk. As he pulled, his skin stretched taut and then distended until the hair ripped out by its roots, and the skin snapped back into place. The closely placed microphone recorded a sound like strips of Velcro being torn apart. Then, as tiny drops of blood began seeping from the follicles of the newly exposed skin, the monk gathered another hank of hair and repeated the process. He tugged his way across his chin and jaw and then went on to the sideburns and head. An hour later, when I walked out, he was still hard at work, with another hour or so to go. As I left, I noted that the women in the darkened room seemed unfazed by the ritual; they were laughing and whispering together, looking relaxed and amused. In stark contrast, the men were scrunched up, like worms on fishing hooks, with their legs squeezed together and their arms crossed defensively across their torsos and laps. I realized that

I had been unconsciously curled into a protective ball too. In many ways, women are tougher than men.

It's easy to see the Jain monks' and nuns' rejection of simple comforts, denial of all ownership, and removal of all hair above the neck as a religious statement. This world offers them no lasting, meaningful pleasures. They do not breed, acknowledge family ties, participate in civic life, or otherwise behave as social mammals (though they rely on others to feed them). One might wonder why they don't also rip out pubic hair while they're at it. The answer, I think, is that they simply prefer to ignore the body, starving its desires by refusing to recognize them. Jain renunciates demonstrate their indifference to their genitals by pretending they aren't there.

## Shaving, rebirth, and shame

World denial is not the only meaning of hair removal, however. Hair can be shaved to indicate rebirth into a new phase of life—as seen in the many Hindu rites of passage—as an offering to Gods, in rituals of mourning, and as a shaming or corrective practice. It can also be used to dehumanize captives, either to remold them, as in military basic training, or to make it easier for otherwise decent human beings to abuse and kill them, as seen so dramatically in the treatment of the shaven prisoners held in Nazi death camps.

One of the most fascinating recent examples of hair shaming is seen in the strange story of Samuel Mullet, the purportedly "iron-fisted" leader of a breakaway sect within the already reclusive Amish faith. Though he is in prison (as of 2015), Bishop Mullet still leads a group of approximately eighteen families, in Bergholz, Ohio, noted for its ultra-strict interpretation of the Amish faith. In 2012 Mullet, then sixty-seven, was convicted of federal hate crimes and conspiracy for orchestrating five nighttime attacks in which his followers broke into the homes of Amish critics, hacking off the men's beards and women's hair with horse shears and electric trimmers. Fifteen of his followers, both male and female, were also found guilty. His goal was to humiliate and shame these fellow Amish, for whom long hair on women and uncut beards for men are of great spiritual significance. The Amish forbid men from growing moustaches but require married men to grow beards, with the end result that they superficially resemble devout Muslims. Following Paul's admonitions in Second Corinthians, Amish men keep their head hair short, but women grow theirs long. Beards for men and long hair for women are essential signs of their obedience to God's commands, so removing the victims' beards and hair took them out of right relationship with the divine and their religious community, even though the cutting was not their choice and obviously beyond their control. Mullet and his gang were judging, sentencing, and punishing their victims, whose disfiguration, while only temporary and largely symbolic, was uniquely humiliating within their closed society.

The religious nature of the beard and hair attacks proved crucial in the trials and was cited by the prosecution as evidence that the attacks were in fact religiously motivated hate crimes. The defendants' lawyers argued that it doesn't make sense to label a crime committed against coreligionists a *religious* hate crime, but this reasoning was not convincing; a great number of religious hate crimes take place within groups against their own members. In general, self-policing tends to be intense in small, exclusive sects where even tiny deviations in theology or practice threaten the sacred unity of the true faith.

The defendants were found guilty and sentenced to terms ranging from a few years to fifteen years in the case of the bishop. The hate crime convictions were overturned on appeal, but other charges were upheld, and Bishop Mullet is still in jail. These crimes are strikingly anomalous for the disciplined, pacifist Amish community. No previous attacks like these have been recorded in the past 320 years of Amish history, though their Anabaptist forbears were not always so well behaved.

It is also noteworthy that the government of the United States recognizes the essential religious significance of long hair and beards for the Amish. The sixteen convicted men and women were allowed to keep their beards and hair in federal prison. It would be wonderfully ironic if they hadn't been, for then the federal government would be committing the very crime for which Mullet and his followers had been convicted!

Not all religious minorities receive such accommodations in prisons, however, especially in state facilities. Muslim men have had to fight to keep their beards in jail, often without success, and Rastafarians' dreadlocks are usually shorn when they are incarcerated. In 2015 a unanimous Supreme Court decision affirmed the right of Muslim prisoners nationwide to grow short beards as a religious duty. (Alabama, Arkansas, Florida, Georgia, South Carolina, Texas, and Virginia have long forbidden beards on all prisoners.) This was a striking ruling, because the courts tend to support the administrative decisions of state prison officials.[15] As a marginalized religious minority, Rastas tend to fare less well, especially in these same southern states. Those Rastas who regrow their hair in prison can be placed in isolation, sometimes for many years, in Virginia at least.[16]

# Early Christianity

Tonsuring is a religious variant of head shaving. The term refers to several styles of radical hair trimming traditional in Western Christianity. It is sometimes used, for lack of a better term, to refer to Asian practices of head shaving, though this can be misleading. Once normative for Roman Catholic monks and friars, tonsuring was banned by the pope in 1972, for general use anyway, but certain strict orders, like the Trappists, have permission to continue the practice. Throughout the medieval and early modern periods tonsuring was standard for any man taking holy orders.

The style runs a range from full head shaving through the Celtic tonsure, the details of which are disputed. The Celtic tonsure may have been a holdover from the Druid priesthood and was attacked as unorthodox by the supporters of the Roman tonsure, or "crown of thorns," where the top and sides of the head are shaved, with a ring of hair left circling the head. The tonsure is often claimed to be the practice of the first generation of Christians in Rome, so its history appears venerable. In practical terms, it made the religious instantly identifiable and may have moderated their behavior in bars, brothels, and other dens of iniquity.

In the early Byzantine Empire, usurpers, deposed emperors, pretenders to the throne, and the like—basically the losers in any serious power struggle—were routinely blinded, which effectively removed them from further contention. By the 700s it became common merely to castrate and tonsure them (and all their sons), sending them into exile or off to monasteries where they were essentially imprisoned. Here the link between castration and head shaving seems painfully clear. We might suggest that the key to the link is found in the involuntary or punitive nature of the act. It seems likely that when prisoners or victims are forcibly shaved, they are, in fact, being symbolically castrated, assuming that they are male. (Women are simply being humiliated and rendered genderless.) In Byzantium, the victors eschewed the subtlety of symbolism and made the link surgically explicit. However, voluntary shaving by adults and the shaving of children's heads should be regarded as holding different symbolic meanings. In some instances, there may be no discernable sexual import; in others there may even be a sex-positive implication.

Priests and monks of the Byzantine, or Eastern Orthodox, Christian tradition usually have their heads and faces shaved when they take holy orders, but then they never cut their hair or shave again. In this case the hair removal seems to mark a change in status, moving from a profane to a sacred state. This is a once-in-a-lifetime transition, so there is no need to repeat the ceremony, and the clerics often grow huge beards. It would be almost impossible to confuse them with clean-shaven, tonsured Catholic priests.

The distinctive hair practices in the two major divisions of early Christianity are not merely a visual key to sectarian affiliation, but appear to have been a factor in the split between the Eastern and Western Churches. Certainly the theological differences between East and West are important, for theologians anyway, as are the divergences in the liturgical calendars and ritual forms, but in the larger scheme of global religions, these differences seem trifling and are far outweighed by the similarities. It was the cumulative weight of many small religious distinctions, as well as ecclesiastic politics, that made the split between East and West unavoidable. When Papal legate Cardinal Humbert and Eastern Orthodox Patriarch Cerularius simultaneously excommunicated each other in 1054, clerical hair was one of many factors underlying the conflict.

# Escape from the planet of emotions, hair, and sex

In the United States, the link between head shaving and castration has been seen as recently as the 1990s, in the new religious movement Heaven's Gate. The forty or so hard-core followers of Marshall Herff Applewhite (1931–97) aspired to ascend to TELAH, "The Evolutionary Level Above Human," a state in which they believed they would be given new bodies, immortal and ageless, transcending the mammalian limits of temporal human existence. In their gnostic worldview, evolution has a teleological thrust leading a select few members of our funky, hairy, biologically driven, ape-like human race to develop into hairless, genderless, emotionless higher beings. It hardly needs mentioning that from their perspective the overwhelming majority of the human race could never be disciplined enough to take this momentous next step.

In the religious imagination of Heaven's Gate, the beings of TELAH look very much like the gray aliens of UFO literature. The "students" of Heaven's Gate believed that by shaving their heads, wearing unisex uniforms, practicing celibacy, communicating in a private, Star Trek-influenced technical dialect, and avoiding all emotional entanglements they were preparing themselves to occupy the genderless, hairless "alien" bodies they would receive when they were picked up by the eagerly anticipated spaceship from the next level.

The most devoted students of Heaven's Gate spent more than two decades working at the exhausting business of transcending all sentiments, all attachments, all personal desires, in order to be ready for the "transit" to the next stage. Once they were safely away, they believed the rest of us on planet earth would be "spaded under."

Those male members of the group who found sexual urges still troubling, despite their great efforts, underwent voluntary surgical castration. (Apparently, it's advisable to go to Mexico for this.) The fact that they shaved their heads and were castrated on their own volition muddies the premise that head shaving and castration are symbolically linked only when they are both involuntary, but that just illustrates the problem with all hair theories. There are exceptions to every rule.

In 1997, thirty-nine members of Heaven's Gate left this world in a mass exit (suicide in society's terms, but "choosing life" in theirs), with the approach of the Hale-Bopp comet. Their website is still maintained, perfectly preserved in its garish 1997 form, by fellow travelers.[17] It's fascinating.

# 4 STYLING

In every epoch for which we have evidence, humans have employed enormous creative energy to devise new and distinctive hairstyles. From braiding to perming to tying hair onto massive wire and wood superstructures, powdering, flouring—before the French revolution put an end to that wasteful practice, French aristocrats purportedly used enough flour on their wigs every month to make thousands of loaves of bread—shaving, sculpting, lacquering, coloring, curling, gilding, waxing, primping, ratting, the list goes on and on.

The styling spectrum is incredibly wide. At one end we see the people who remove all their hair and at the other those who refuse to cut or pluck a single strand. The subject is so enormous it can scarcely be summarized, much less comprehensively analyzed. What we'll do is look at a few examples, presented within their historical contexts and ranging widely over time and geography, to see what trends emerge.

One point most authors repeat is that hair cutting, like head shaving, is generally associated with control, especially when hair is cut very short. This control can be imposed by an external force—parents, society, the military, prison officials, religious regulations—or it may be an expression of self-discipline. As generalizations go, this one is uncontroversial and safe, as it generally holds up under scrutiny. On the other end, long uncut hair—if tightly bound, braided, coiled, or covered—can also be a sign of conservative control, but if left flowing wild, it is almost always seen as rebellious, feral, and destructive (or contemptuous) of social order. Long hair can be trouble, at least for the guardians of social and religious orthodoxy. Libertines and rebels, outlaws and antinomians all favor long, loose hair. It's bad for the status quo, and it's often bad for business.

## "Savage" hair

The first European colonists who settled the New World were baffled by the American Indians.[1] Who were they? How did they get to this far-off continent? (Remember the first settlers were Bible-believing literalists. They knew their creation stories, and they realized that if biblical history is true, there is a problem accounting for the Indians.) They found native ways frightening, and they accused the Indians of witchcraft and demon worship, assuming them guilty until proven otherwise. They were also shocked by the indigenous peoples' hair.

Despite not having scissors or metal tweezers, American Indians were able to do amazing things with their hair, plucking their bodies and shaving their scalps in intricate patterns using just shells and stone tools. (Copper tweezers only appeared after the arrival of the first Europeans.) Men often removed or tied back hair that could interfere with bow use, and many tribes fashioned elaborate scalp locks that were highly prized by their wearers. Having your scalp lock hacked off by an enemy was a great dishonor. Animal fat, powdered rocks, floral essences, skins, feathers, and more were used to style and perfume hair, which could be stiffened into elaborate crests. Judging from the panic the punks created with their dyed and sprayed Mohawks—really pretty tame for the ostensibly cosmopolitan, globalized twentieth century—it's hard to imagine how distressed the colonists must have felt when first encountering their new neighbors!

Reconstructing the meanings of precontact hairstyles is a challenge. The records are incomplete, and most of the information we have comes from explorers who were sometimes acute observers, but who carried presuppositions and cultural baggage we can scarcely imagine. Obviously they had no intention of creating anthropological databases when recording their notes. Still we can learn from the analysis of early records. Some of the best descriptions of first-contact Indian hair were made of the Powhatan, a federation of thirty tribes in the tidewater region of Virginia. In her article "Powhatan Hair," Margaret Holmes Williamson analyzes accounts written soon after the founding of the Jamestown Colony in 1607.

Williamson argues that the three distinctive hairstyles worn by the Powhatan were clear markers of gender and religious standing. Unmarried women shaved the front and sides of their heads but wore the rest of their hair long, their trailing punkish mullets denoting their status as fully feminine and potentially available. Married women favored bowl cuts, still feminine if matronly. (Williamson counts these two hairstyles as one.)

Commoner men and chiefs shaved the right half of their scalps, ostensibly to aid in shooting bows, while tying the long hair on the left and decorating it with copper ornaments and other "Gewgawes, as . . . the hand of their Enemy dryed."[2] Despite the badass ferocity displayed by men who perk up their "do" with mummified human hands, Williamson claims that commoners and chiefs alike revealed their dual-natured male/female polarity with their contrasting half-shaven, half-long hair. Her reasoning is complex but comes down to the hypothesis that the only fully male Powhatans were the shamans, who shaved both sides of their heads, preserving a thin forehead-to-nape strip of hair shaped into an upright crest resembling the Mohawk on the cover of this book. Shamans were also the only Powhatans allowed to grow beards, which for Williamson secures their status as fully male. Curiously, the shamans were not allowed to marry and lived apart from society, not even speaking to commoners of either gender, so the only truly "male" Powhatans were recluses who were either celibate or gay.

The main problem with this analysis is that the Powhatans never endorsed it, nor were their surviving descendants consulted to see if they preserved lore explaining their ancestors' hair. What is clear, however, is that the Powhatans were signaling *something* with their hair, at least to other members of their group. Whether neighboring tribes employed similar stylistic conventions is uncertain, though likely. The American Indians' vocabulary of hair was extraordinarily rich, nuanced, and complex. While we assume there must have been some continuities between tribes, mutually intelligible dialects of symbolic meanings, my American Indian students have always reminded me that tribal cultures were distinct, even unique. They find the generalizations repeated in textbooks to be offensive and misleading.

When I was in graduate school, I became fascinated by the long and unusual career of John Eliot (1604–90), "Apostle to the Indians." Eliot first gained notoriety as one of the ministers active in the heresy trial of Anne Hutchinson. To be fair, he played a minor role and was the least aggressive prosecutor.

What made him truly distinctive, however, was his surprising openness on "racial" issues. Unlike many of his Calvinist brethren, Eliot was convinced that the indigenous peoples of the Americas had souls and could be led to Christ. While his fellow Puritans favored extermination as the most expeditious way to gain more land, Eliot disagreed. He believed that the Indians could be saved, both physically and spiritually, by large-scale conversion to Christianity. To that end, Eliot researched native languages, composing a number of prayers in Algonquin and eventually translating the entire Bible into Massachusett, a related language, in 1663—the first Bible printed in the Colonies.

What is most striking about Elliot's mission were the steps he took to "Christianize" the Indians. Elliot was convinced that the Indians must stop hunting and gathering their food. Farming was the Christian way. He believed that the Indians had far too much fun running about freely, without fixed abode and regular daily chores. They needed to live in cabins, keep animals, farm their fields, and follow set routines. So, he settled his flock in villages—eventually establishing fourteen communities—and schooled them in the tedium of English yeoman farmers, in his mind the way of all true Christians. These steps were essential for conversion, but not sufficient. Above all, their hair needed to be controlled.[3]

During the English Civil War (starting in 1642) the plain-styled Puritans were derided as "Roundheads," a pejorative term coined to mock the short-cropped hair many of them adopted. This contrasted with their enemies, the aristocratic Royalist "Cavaliers," who characteristically flaunted foppishly long, curled hair. Perhaps Eliot was influenced by events in the home country and the negative European stereotype of the vain, longhaired aristocrat when he laid down the rules for his new converts. Perhaps he simply believed that the Protestant faith and short hair were inextricably linked. In any case, he seemed far more concerned with the hair of his converts than their actual religious beliefs.

In his writings, Eliot returned almost obsessively to the Indians' hair. It was long, way too long. Even worse,

Indians personalized their hair; they adopted individual styles. Eliot was absolutely convinced that they needed rigidly standardized British Puritan haircuts, both to make them identifiably Christian in the eyes of his less accepting coreligionists, and because he appeared to think that hair really made a religious difference. Longhaired Indians were uncivilized, wild, dangerous, and unsaved. Christians had short hair. When Eliot's converts rebelled against boring new lives as pseudo-English peasants—this happened far too frequently it seems—the first thing they did was stop cutting their hair. Before long, they were back to their devilish, un-Christian lifestyle of hunting, fishing, and running about in the deep forest, the demonic "howling wilderness" that haunted Puritan nightmares.

So perhaps Eliot was right.

## Christian women's modesty

While Western Christianity has usually preferred short hair for men, from its inception, Christianity has mandated long, uncut, but controlled hair for women. Paul's famous claim that a woman's hair is her glory has often been cited as the source for the custom, but it's known that women had long hair in the Mediterranean region many centuries before the Christian era. In most historical periods this long hair has been covered for modesty, both in religious settings and in public spaces. Women with loose, long hair were assumed to be wanton and immoral, and because everyone knew and followed the rules, and society's control was largely unchallenged, the assumption was often self-fulfilling. Though Islam is now commonly seen as the primary religion requiring women to cover their hair, this is a modern development. In the past, the practice was widespread. Hair covering and veiling of women were traditional upper-class practices throughout the Middle East, and Christians were as enthusiastic in mandating these behaviors as any of their neighbors. Up until the last century or so, respectable women in many parts of the world covered their hair in public. Free flowing hair has only become acceptable recently, and in the United States we still see the traditional covering of long female hair upheld by the Amish, Mennonites, Pentecostals, and other conservative Christian groups. Even now we can see lingering traces of obligatory women's hair covering in largely secular events like the Kentucky Derby. The talk may be of fashion or skin cancer, but religious traditions are the ancient underlying force.

## Good hair

We should now glance at the fascinating topic of African-American hair, knowing that many volumes would be needed to do it justice. Ever since the dark days of American slavery, persons of recent African descent (as opposed to the rest of us, who have more distant African origins) have been distinguished, and in some ways even defined, by their hair. Usually kinky or curly, African-American hair has been approached in varying ways: with shame, pride, ambivalence, acceptance, and many shades of nuance. It has tended to function as an identifier, with kinkier hair seen as more "African," and straighter hair as more "white." African-American women spend fortunes on weaves and wigs, and a flourishing hair-care industry provides various treatments to straighten African-American hair. Many of the older straightening concoctions contain lye and other caustic ingredients that make them as harsh and painful as the depilatory potions of the medieval Islamic world. If left on too long, some of them will, in fact, remove the hair they are supposed to straighten.

The significance and subtle meanings of African-American hairstyles have been analyzed at great length in a number of scholarly articles; we could not begin to do them justice here. It's a fascinating subfield of study. Anyone interested in a popular introduction to the subject might want to start with Chris Rock's engaging and entertaining documentary *Good Hair* (2009). If you aren't yet a fan of Mr. Rock, you should be after watching this humorous, insightful film.

Salons in several parts of the United States experienced a rash of hair thefts in 2011; many thousands of dollars in wigs, weaves, and "virgin hair" from India were stolen. It was suggested that *Good Hair* should take part of the blame, for alerting criminals to the big money to be made selling "hot" hair.[4] If the blame is legitimate, it suggests that Mr. Rock's work appeals to a diverse demographic.

In June 2015, a flurry of media stories addressed the strange story of Rachel Dolezal, a blond-haired, fair-skinned white woman who not only passed as black but also became a respected civil rights activist, rising to the presidency of the National Association for the Advancement of Colored People (NAACP) in Spokane, Washington. Reporters and editorialists instantly took aim at her, expressing outrage, embarrassment, astonishment, and more. The question of *why* Ms. Dolezal identified as African-American is psychologically complex, but the *how* is straightforward: her hair. Although she did something to darken her skin—perhaps as simple as a bit of spray tan—the basis of the deception, the factor that made it work, was her dyed and permed hair. As Martha Jones, chair of African-American Studies at the University of Michigan, told the *Chronicle of Higher Education*:

> She's been reading our scholarship and our commentary. She knows if there's an intervention to be made in terms of her presentation of self, it's the hair. We all read each other, write about hair, and there's a whole lit[erature] about the significance, power, and symbolism of hair for black women. She knows that hair transforms the way we are read. Rachel is a really astute student of race in a curious way.[5]

It's ironic that Ms. Dolezal took great efforts to make her hair look "black," while generations of African Americans have worked at least as hard to make their hair look "white." Everyone seems to share the same understanding of the power of hair to create identity.

Rather than address African hair in general, a massive undertaking, we will look at two contrasting extremes on the religious and tonsorial spectrum: the hairstyles of the Rastafari and the Nation of Islam.

# Rastafari

The religion of Rastafari began in Jamaica in the 1930s as a back-to-the-land countercultural movement, originally appealing to the economically disadvantaged and generally less well-educated segments of the African-Caribbean majority. Since that time, the movement has become far more mainstream and demographically diverse, with a number of distinguished scholarly advocates and middle-class followers. Because the movement started in Jamaica, it is often assumed that orthodox Jamaican beliefs and practices are normative for all dreadlocked "Rastas." This is questionable. Rastafari has always been a diverse movement, and many related groups, such as the "Dreads" of Dominica, diverge significantly in theology from their Jamaican cousins. With that caveat, we will look briefly at the Jamaican roots of Rastafari.

The movement was inspired in part by Marcus Garvey (1887–1940), a black Jamaican intellectual, politician, journalist, and entrepreneur. Garvey accomplished a great deal in his wide-ranging career as an inspiring orator, writer, and businessman, including founding a pioneering Pan-African organization, the Universal Negro Improvement Association (UNIA), and creating the Black Star Line, a shipping company many Jamaicans believed would repatriate them to their homeland in Africa. Garvey's teachings on African unity, his dream of an all-black civilization in Africa, and his insistence on the need for black self-sufficiency and economic independence inspired a wide range of movements, including the Rastafari, many sects of which view Garvey as a prophet, and the Nation of Islam. Central to the founding myth of the Rastafari is the belief that Garvey prophesied, "Look to Africa, when a black king shall be crowned, for the day of deliverance is at hand!" (The wording of this prophecy varies with the source and no definitive version can be established.)

When Prince Rastafari Makonnen was crowned emperor of Ethiopia in 1930, assuming the title of Haile Selassie I, a number of Jamaicans believed that Garvey's prophecy had been fulfilled. Their savior had appeared. For Jamaican Rastas, Haile Selassie I, or Jah (short for Jehovah) as he is usually called, is the living Lord, "the God Head, The Ancient of Days," despite the fact that throughout his life he professed to be an Ethiopian Orthodox Christian.[6]

The Rastafari movement, originally focusing on Haile Selassie as the redeemer promised in the Bible, got off to a humble start in rural Jamaica during the 1930s. A number of distinctive practices gradually developed. The ceremonial use of ganja (a Hindi name for marijuana, suggesting possible South Asian influences) alarmed the civil authorities, and the growth of beards drew early distain from nearly all segments of Jamaican society. Though Rastas are now best known for their dreadlocks—long, tangled mats of hair—in the early years of the movement, beards were the identifying feature of Rastas. Beards cost them their jobs, leading to communal self-sufficiency and the development of a thriving crafts and small business economy.

As the Rastas studied the Bible in greater depth, many concluded that dreadlocks were divinely ordained. By the early 1960s, Rastas were divided over the issue of hair, with three factions—the neatly trimmed "combheads," the "beard men," and the dread wearers—disputing the modern applicability of the Nazirite vows and the religious necessity of growing dreads.[7] To this day there are surviving old-school Rastas who have not adopted dreadlocks, though nearly all wear beards.

White Jamaicans viewed dreadlocks with fear, seeing them as a symbol of the wild uncivilized temper of their wearers, while Jamaicans of color tended to see beards and dreadlocks as rustic and unsophisticated, an embarrassing rejection of the pains respectable people took to look "presentable."

In the small, overwhelmingly black Caribbean nation of Dominica, dreadlocks provoked more than distain. A draconian law known as the Dread Act was passed in 1974, authorizing police to arrest dreadlocked individuals on sight, without a warrant, and mandating prison terms for wearing dreads. Dreadlock wearers usually served nine-month sentences, just for their hair. Further, the law exonerated policemen who happened to shoot "Dreads" and authorized the general public to shoot on sight any Dreads found "inside a dwelling house," a strangely ambiguous provision that even Dominicans find puzzling. This act was perhaps the harshest instance of governmental religious persecution in the West since 1838, when Missouri Executive Order 44 authorized the extermination and/or expulsion of all Mormons from the state of Missouri. While Executive Order 44 was only in force for a few days, the Dread Act stayed on the books until 1984! By this time, hundreds of Dominican Dreads had endured prison and several dozen had been shot. Curiously many of these early Dominican Dreads did not believe in the divinity of Haile Selassie and did not call themselves Rastas, though their natural, agrarian lifeways, ceremonial use of ganja, and hairstyles were largely indistinguishable from the practices of the orthodox Jamaican Rastafari.[8]

For Rastas who wear dreads, their matted hair is biblical, and they justify their appearance by citing the rules for Nazirites, as given in Numbers 6:1-21, and the injunction given in Leviticus 19:27, "Do not cut the hair at the sides of your head or clip off the edges of your beard." (This rule also gives us the side curls worn by ultraorthodox Jewish men.) In addition to being ordained by God, dreadlocks are natural. Dreads are a rejection of the processing and the labor-intensive grooming efforts that are a legacy of slave culture; they affirm the Africanness of their wearers. Dreadlocks symbolize freedom and mental liberation, with Rastas noting that cut and combed hair leads to well-ordered, unimaginative, conventional thinking, while dreads are a sign and even cause of unfettered mental and spiritual freedom. Most Rastas avoid unnatural chemical concoctions like soap and shampoo, cleaning their dreads with herbal infusions. Female Rastas also wear dreads, but they usually cover their hair when they go out, so their dreads are rarely seen in public. Male Rastas sometimes cover their dreads as well, to keep them clean and to avoid getting them caught or damaged. Like the Sikhs, who also leave their hair uncut, many Rasta believe that hair is alive, bearing little resemblance to the dead protein strands described by scientists.

Before the phenomenal global success of reggae music and the huge popularity of Bob Marley, dreads were not particularly widespread among non-Rastas. Now, of course, dreadlocks are seen worldwide. In 1993, I was astonished to see a Chinese man in rural Yunnan, in the far southwest of China, with impressive dreads. White college students in the United States often cultivate dreads as well, investing considerable time and money to force straight Euro hair into tangled locks; however, few of these young wearers seem to follow the teachings of Rastafari. For them, dreads are a fashion statement and often carry little or no religious meaning, though they may suggest the wearers' musical tastes.

# Nation of Islam

Like the Rastafari, the Nation of Islam (NOI) also believes that a black man is God, in this case not Haile Selassie I but a mysterious carpet and silk salesman named W. D. Fard. Nothing certain is known about Master Fard's life before his appearance in Detroit in 1930, and his disappearance in 1934 has never been explained. He appears to have vanished off the face of the earth. Much like Jesus, everything we know of Master Fard is based on a few years of public teaching. (Curiously, in the few known photographs of Fard, he looks more European, or possibly Middle Eastern, than black.)

Elijah Muhammad (born Elijah Poole, 1897–1975), Fard's most ardent disciple, led the Nation of Islam from 1934 until his death in 1975. Elijah Muhammad is responsible for a number of distinctive teachings in the NOI, teachings that move the religion far away from Islamic orthodoxy. Perhaps the most non-Islamic teachings of the NOI are the claims that W. D. Fard is Allah, God on earth, and that Elijah Muhammad is a prophet. Orthodox Muslims categorically reject both these assertions. In Islam, Allah never takes human form, and Muhammad was the last of the prophets; there can be no prophets after him.

Elijah Muhammad's revelations also introduce elements of science fiction to the faith, as seen in his descriptions of the "Mother Wheel," an enormous spacecraft made by black scientists that is hiding from view within our solar system, and his claim that a mad black scientist created white people, through a eugenics program, six thousand years ago on the island of Patmos. Scholars suggest that the NOI is as much a UFO-based new religious movement as an offshoot of Islam.[9]

After Elijah Muhammad's death, his son, W. D. Muhammad, who had studied Arabic and traditional Sunni Islam, took over the organization and began leading the following to orthodox Sunni Muslim teachings and practices. This necessarily led to the refutation of many of his father's most distinctive teachings. Not all members of the NOI were happy with this dramatic reorientation of their religion.

A disaffected splinter group, led by Louis Farrakhan, returned to the original teaching of Elijah Muhammad and restored the NOI in 1978. The revived NOI embraces Elijah Muhammad's teachings of black separatism, while continuing to emphasize hard work, clean living, sobriety, personal dignity, and traditional gender roles. In line with the strong traditional ethical teachings of the NOI, the faithful are noted for the precision of their grooming. Men keep their hair cropped extremely short, often wearing dark suits and bow ties, while women usually wear long dresses and cover their heads with scarves to preserve their modesty. So although the religious teachings of the NOI are in many ways radically inventive, the hairstyles of the followers project conservative values and firm self-control. The clean-cut, dignified members of the NOI outdo in grooming and deportment the white society they reject, embracing a notion of spiritualized Africanness that is highly disciplined and structured. This puts them in sharp contrast to the Rastas' dreadlocked Africanness, which is natural, organic, rural, unfettered, and wild. As different as the Rastas and the NOI appear in theology and hairstyles, both owe a great debt to Marcus Garvey.

## Passage to India

Let's now move on to India, one of the great traditional centers of hair manipulation. For most of Indian history, ordinary villagers of the lower three *varna* (commonly called "castes" in English) kept their hair neat, clean, and oiled. Both sexes might have their heads shaved during important rituals and for periods of mourning, but it was normal to let shaven hair regrow.

Hindu males were traditionally distinguished by the *shikha*, a single tuft of hair at the top/back/center of the head, a few inches behind the fontanel. The shikha was often tied into a knot when in public. It is now seen mostly on Brahmin temple priests and hard-core religious conservatives, many of whom are also Brahmins. Brahmins who pursue secular work in the cities have largely dropped the style. It looks embarrassingly stogy and old fashioned in India's business and professional worlds. (Of course, it looks totally punk and antiestablishment in the West!) Nowadays, most Hindu men have short, neat hair, and in the South a very high percentage grow moustaches.

Brahmin wives traditionally wore their long hair in tight braids. A Brahmin woman unfortunate enough to be widowed was expected to shave her head, which is standard mourning practice in India, but then she was required to remain shaven-headed for the rest of her life—dressing exclusively in white, the color of celibacy and death, as well—to signify that she was done with sex forever. (Hindu widowers, however, are free to remarry.)

Widows also bore the blame and shame for their husbands' deaths. (In rural areas they still do.) Wives who are astrologically favored and sufficiently pious should be able to keep their husbands healthy for long, full lives. Should a husband die before his wife, it is obviously her fault. While their husbands are alive, traditional Brahmin wives are expected to spend at least three days a month fasting and performing rituals believed to ensure their husbands' longevity. It's easy to see why they might take this duty seriously.

It's fascinating that ritual head shaving before marriage marks an orthodox Jewish woman's official entry into the world of sex and reproduction, while the shaving of a widowed Brahmin woman marks her exit. In each context, Jewish and Hindu, shaven heads clearly signal women's sexual/reproductive standings in society, but the meanings conveyed by the hairless heads are diametrically opposed. The drama is unmistakable, as is the violence, but the significance and consequences could not be more different.

Women from lower castes were often spared the humiliation of lifelong head shaving and wearing of white. In general, the lower the caste ranking, the more likely widows were to keep their hair. Some were even allowed to remarry.

In India, because shaving usually signifies and celebrates transitions, it can therefore carry positive, life-affirming meanings as well as the expected ones of life-negation. A few years ago, my wife and I visited a low caste village temple in Tamil Nadu noted for its hair shaving rituals. We were taken there by a mischievous informant, a self-identified Marxist with an anthropology degree, who hoped to shock us with what he considered the scandalous underbelly of Hindu society. Removing our shoes, we walked several hundred feet into the temple grounds, our feet squishing and sticking on the paving stones, black with filth. Huge mats of flies paved the courtyard, swarming out from under our descending feet as we walked, settling back in our wake. After admiring the severed heads of two freshly sacrificed goats, we were taken to a dark concrete chamber, where a barber squatted, shaving the head of a naked little boy, perhaps three years old. Hindu children's heads are usually shaved for the first time at the age of either one or three; a popular belief is that hair carries karmic impressions from the child's past life, and this first hair cutting frees the child from those influences. The boy's mother then washed the child off under a nearby tap and rubbed a thick yellow paste made of turmeric and water over his scalp. The boy did not cry, despite the potentially traumatizing nature of his ordeal, which is a good sign. He'll face many more symbolic shavings in his life, and even death, since corpses traditionally receive a full body shave before cremation.

As we have already seen, some sadhus, Indian religious renunciates, shave their heads and faces, others go for complete neglect, letting hair, beard, and nails grow as long as possible. Both extremes express the sadhus' rejection of sex and family responsibilities.

Conservative Vaishnavas, Hindu devotees of Vishnu and his avatars, still shave most of their heads, leaving just a *shikha*, or single tuft of hair at the top/back of the head. This is the classic Brahmin hairstyle discussed above. In the West, you can see this hairstyle on members of the International Society for Krishna Consciousness (ISKCON), known popularly as "Hare Krishnas." The Hare Krishnas are a branch of Gaudiya (Bengali) Vaishnavism noted for its elevation of Krishna, one of the incarnations of Vishnu, to the position of Supreme Being.

Not only does the shikha resonate with punk fashion in the West, the Hare Krishnas have had some success propagating their faith among members of the straight-edge punk subculture, who often appreciate the antidrug, anti-alcohol, anti-meat, anti-materialism, and anti-sex message of ISKCON. There is even a global subgenre of Hare Krishna punk music called "Krishna-core," well documented on YouTube. As my late mother might say, it's *"interesting."*

According to Hare Krishna informants, the shikha marks its wearers as devotees of the one true God, Krishna. ISKCON members have told me, only half in jest, that when pure devotees die, Krishna pulls their eternal souls up to Vaikuntha, his heavenly planet, by grasping their shikhas. More seriously, it is thought that back when Buddhists and Jains were still common in India, shikhas functioned to distinguish Hindu theists from "non-theists," the shaven-headed Buddhists and hand-plucked Jains: one savior god/ one tuft; no savior gods/no hair.

Hare Krishnas also hold a Hindu minority position that believes the Buddha was an incarnation of Vishnu—and therefore a god—not a human being who had found the path to salvation or nirvana. Their claim, then, is that the Buddha was an avatar of Vishnu who came to earth to spread the false teaching that gods should not be worshiped and cannot save their followers. Why did he do this? His purpose in taking human birth was to steer the faithless and undeserving away from true religion, thus ensuring their perdition.

When I taught middle school in rural Georgia, back in the 1970s, many of my students attributed similarly devious motives to the God of the Bible. With childlike innocence, my sixth-grade pupils assured me that God had forged the fossil record 6,000 years ago, when he was creating the world, in order to lead wavering souls astray. Both of these stories of divine deceit strike me as excessive, underhanded, and quite unnecessary. Surely there are already sufficient forces of skepticism in the world without an omniscient, sneaky divinity actively promoting disbelief.

# "There is no Hindu and no Muslim"

The Sikh ("disciples") tradition arose in the Panjab (Punjab) of Northwest India in the 1500s, a time of low-level, continuous conflict between Islamic rulers and their largely Hindu subjects. While the religious tensions were significant, it was also a time of creative synthesis. New forms of worship and religious music developed, stimulated by the cross fertilization of Sufi Muslim devotionalism with related Hindu bhakti movements.

Nanak (1469–1539), now called Guru Nanak, the founder of the Sikh religion, was one of those great religious prodigies that India produces by the score. His spiritual talents were obvious even in his childhood. When he was thirty, he received a revelation that started him on his path as a guru, or religious teacher. Emerging after a mysterious three-day disappearance, during which he was assumed to have drowned in a local river, Nanak announced, "There is no Hindu and no Muslim, so whose path should I follow? I will follow God's path." With this anti-sectarian claim, he began his religious outreach. By the time of his death, his reformist movement was in full stride. A series of nine successor gurus continued to spread the faith and organize the religion, until the last, Gobind Singh, declared that the line of human gurus had ended; from that point on the Sikhs' sole guru would be the Adi Granth, their sacred text.

In a time of clear demarcations between Hindus and Muslims, each wearing clothes and hairstyles that established their religious identity in a glance, Nanak was noted for his multi-sectarian attire; his apparel was a mixture of items traditionally worn by either Hindu or Muslim holy men, but never both, making his affiliation impossible to discern. It did not appear that he was creating a new competing tradition but rather harmonizing the two currently dominant, antagonistic faiths.

Consequently, many outside observers have seen the Sikh tradition as a skillful remix of the best beliefs and practices of Hinduism and Islam. While this is plausible, it is not the understanding of the Sikhs themselves. They see their religion as a distinctive new revelation that presents the Truth, parts of which were revealed in earlier belief systems.

In the first two centuries of the faith, the Sikh tradition continued to evolve. Under the nine human gurus who came after Nanak, new texts were added to the early versions of the Adi Granth, beliefs became standardized, worship centers—or *gurdwaras*—were built, and the faithful began to organize for self-defense. The latter was needed. The Sikhs faced persecution at the hands of Muslim rulers who felt so threatened by this new movement that they tortured and murdered several of the Sikh gurus.

Gobind Singh, the tenth and last guru, had clearly had enough. He abolished the chain of human gurus, and in 1699 established the khalsa, a military order within the Sikh faith that would soon earn enormous respect for its martial discipline and ferocity in battle. The khalsa was, and is, open to both men and women, all of whom discard their caste upon initiation, in theory at least, and who adopt the "5 Ks," distinctive grooming and apparel that make khalsa Sikhs immediately identifiable in society and especially in the heat of battle. (In Punjabi, the names of the 5Ks all start with the letter K.) Not all Sikhs are members of the khalsa.

The first K is *kesh*, or hair. Khalsa Sikhs are never supposed to cut, trim, tweeze, dye, or alter any hair, anywhere on the body, in any way. Nose hair, ear hair, facial hair, pubic hair, all hair is sacred, bestowed by the divine, and never to be removed or modified. At the same time, the Sikhs place great emphasis on dignity and cleanliness, so their hair is always kept clean, well combed, and, for men, covered with a turban.

The second of the Ks is *kangh*, or comb, and khalsa Sikhs always carry or wear a comb (often under the turban, stuck in the hair like an Afro pick.) Sikh hair can get amazingly long, perhaps because of those excellent South Asian hair genes, or perhaps because of the way it is pampered.

To illustrate: When my daughters were young they had a Sikh friend who always wore his hair bound up in a turban. Naturally, my daughters wanted to see it, though the boy's mother demurred. Once, when we adults were busy in conversation, my daughters charmed their friend into removing his turban. When first unfurled, his hair came respectably to the middle of his back. By the time we discovered them, my daughters had finished combing it out. We were amazed to see that his hair, fully extended, reached nearly to his knees. It was stunning.

Sikhs strongly oppose body modifications like circumcision, because they believe the body is perfect just as the creator made it. Needless to say, when the neighboring Muslims were removing armpit and pubic hair, shaving moustaches, circumcising males, and dyeing beards with henna, the Sikh no-tamper rule made members of the khalsa readily identifiable. It was also impossible for members of the khalsa to fade into the background in battle; their appearance made their allegiance unmistakable. Sikhs are also forbidden to eat Muslim halal or Jewish kosher meat. If, as some claim, the religion was originally focused on harmonizing regional faiths and practices, by the time the khalsa was formed the Sikhs were determined to emphasize differences.

Most Sikh converts were originally Hindus who brought a long cultural history of ritual head shaving to their new faith. While growing long hair was acceptable to most converts, a controversy soon arose regarding the dead. Hindus believed that corpses must be shaved before cremation; Sikh elders determined that this was unacceptable (Sikhs are commonly cremated, though burial on land or disposal at sea are permissible.). Hair must never be cut, even after death. This prohibition also included the traditional Indian practice of head shaving for the bereaved during times of mourning.

These hair rules were so disturbing to some new converts that they left the faith.

In 2014, a young female khalsa member named Harnaam Kaur created a media stir when photographs of her facial hair appeared on multiple Internet sites where they were viewed by millions. Apparently, Ms. Kaur developed polycystic ovary syndrome when she was a teen and as a result began growing heavy facial hair. She went through a predictable teen crisis, trying many methods of depilation but still being bullied horribly. When she joined the khalsa, she finally found closure and accepted her moustache and beard as God's will. A few years later, when her photographs hit the Internet, she was attacked by the usual array of trolls. She responded with a compelling plea for self-acceptance, tolerance, and respect for our bodies just as the divine created them, largely silencing her critics.

The incredible resistance and bullying she encountered illustrates how vehemently humans respond to violations of their gender expectations. Facial hair, a purely male gender trait, must not be seen on women. We have already encountered an apocalyptic response to the trope of the woman with heavy facial hair, in the Iranian folk belief that a bearded woman preaching in a masjid will signal the end of the world. One suspects these emotional responses are hardwired, and their learned cultural components merely supplement their strength.

The khalsa Sikhs' appearance identifies them clearly and unambiguously in India. Their full moustaches, extravagant beards and often enormous turbans—their head hair occupies a lot of space—distinguish them from short-haired, heavily moustachioed, beardless Hindus, bearded but moustache-lite Muslims, and Hindu sadhus with either shaved heads or long, tangled, free-range hair. They have created an unmistakable look and marked out a unique niche within the contested field of Indian hair. Unfortunately, the rest of the world shows little understanding of India's rigorous hair codes. In the United States, Sikhs are frequent victims of attacks directed against Muslims, their long-term antagonists. It is a bizarre twist. After firmly rejecting Muslim apparel and tonsorial norms and creating their own distinctive look, Sikhs still get identified as Muslims. It's as weird as if Mohawk-crested pierced punks were consistently mistaken for Deadheads.

In 2012 Sikhs in Oak Creek, Wisconsin were victims of a terrorist massacre inflicted by a discharged Army psychological operations soldier. The ex-soldier killed six Sikhs at their gurdwara, injuring nine more, before being shot in the stomach by a responding officer, and then killing himself. He left no note, so his motives are uncertain. It has been speculated that he thought he was attacking Muslims, though it is possible he was simply targeting non-European Americans. If, in fact, he saw the turbans and thought he was killing Muslims, then he was not just a homicidal bigot but also an idiot, given that Sikhs are the only significant turban-wearing group in America. (Muslims almost never wear turbans in the West.) You then have to wonder about his training in the Army. What was he taught? Did he learn nothing of the vocabulary of hair? Although Rastafari women and a few members of new religious movements may wear turbans as part of their spiritual practice, they are exceedingly rare. If you see a man wearing a turban in the West, you can be nearly positive you've spotted a khalsa Sikh.

The Sikhs are one of the most visible religions to use hair and dress to differentiate themselves from Muslims, but many other religions, large and small, have created hair practices that distinguish their followers from Muslims. For example, the priests of the critically endangered Mandaean religion, a gnostic Middle Eastern monotheistic faith that reveres John the Baptist, never shave their head hair. Instead, they weave their hair into a gigantic braid that they coil on top of their heads and cover with a turban.[10] The Mandaeans also assert that salvation is not possible for circumcised men. While their teachings show clear affinities with the Judeo-Christian-Islamic traditions, the Mandaeans have made it certain they won't be mistaken for Muslims, or Jews for that matter.

## The Celestial Kingdom

In traditional Chinese culture, men wore their hair long and secured in a knot at the top of their heads, often held with a hairpin. The head was then covered with a cap, so that the hair knot was concealed. Men let their hair down only in private. In their public lives, they wore caps that clearly signaled their social status, business or trade, and educational level.

Members of the different trades and guilds were marked by their distinctive caps or hats, as were beggars. Men who had passed various grades of the civil service exams proclaimed their ranks with the emblems on their hats. Confucian society placed a premium on knowing one's place, and that could only be established in comparison with others. Fortunately, an astute reader of the signs could always determine his or her relative rank in any social interaction, thereby preserving harmony. Hats made this possible.

Confucius also taught the importance of relationships between generations. Fathers had responsibilities to their offspring, and in turn children owed obedience to their parents. One of the most important ways children repaid their debts to their parents was by preserving the bodies their parents had given them. For this reason, Confucians loathed tattoos and other forms of body modification, for even if your parents were no longer on earth to see the dishonor you had done to them by marking your body, they would find out soon enough—you appear in the afterlife just as you do at your death. The Imperial Chinese state was therefore especially fond of mutilation as a deterrent and punishment for criminal actions—facial tattoos, nose removal, branding, caning, and the like were favorites. Criminals were disfigured not just in this life but the next as well.

When the Manchu "barbarian" invaders solidified their control over China and established the Qing dynasty (1644–1911), one of their first demands was that Chinese men adopt the Manchu hairstyle, on pain of death. Confucians were horrified. The Manchu hairstyle, commonly called the queue, made good sense for nomadic warriors. The front half of the head was shaved bare and the remaining hair was braided into a long pigtail that hung down in back. The queue ensured unobstructed vision in the heat of battle, so it was practical in war and on horseback, but it looked uncivilized and absurd to the Chinese. To adopt such an outlandish hairstyle would be treason, or so the Chinese reasoned. It would be a betrayal of their emperor, their venerable civilization, and their ancestors. Even worse, as the hairstyle of barbarous conquerors, it looked stupid. Tens of thousands of Chinese men chose to be executed rather than shave their foreheads and adopt the queue, presumably going to meet their ancestors with their honor, hair, and fashion sense intact.

Over the long centuries of Manchu rule, the conquering "barbarians" were culturally overwhelmed by the power, depth, and refinement of Chinese civilization. The Manchus' customs, clothing, manners, and even language were slowly forgotten; by the late twentieth century only a few elderly women still spoke Manchu. Yet the queue outlived all other facets of Manchu culture, surviving until the very last days of their empire.

Throughout the Qing dynasty, Chinese rebels launched attacks against the Manchu overlords and their Chinese collaborators. There were many causes of rebellion, of course. Starvation, social injustice, and economic hardship fueled many short-lived revolts. Nativist movements hoping to expel the foreign overlords had some appeal, as well, but the only rebellions with real staying power were religious. If a rebellion lasted long enough for the rebels to grow out their hair, they invariably did. Even after centuries of forced tonsorial uniformity, the Chinese identified long hair with traditional Chinese culture and civilization. Growing hair out was a rejection of the Manchus' barbarian customs and a repudiation of their illegitimate rule.

By far the most serious challenge to the Qing dynasty came from the Taiping (太平 "Great Peace") movement in the middle of the nineteenth century. In retrospect the name is cruelly ironic, for more than twenty million people died before the rebellion was crushed. The movement illustrates the dangers inherent in exporting a dualistic, millennial religion—in this case Christianity—without proper warning labels. Among other things, new converts tend to be judgmental literalists and fanatics who believe that ancient commandments should be followed to the letter, not tempered by reason, scholarship, or centuries of tradition. The movement started out well enough, however, with the visionary flights of a frustrated examination candidate named Hong Xiuquan (1814–64).

Like many bright boys, Hong was selected by his family to study for the grueling imperial exams. Success in the exams was the traditional Chinese equivalent of winning the lottery; honor and riches would come to the candidate's entire family. Unfortunately, as many aspiring scholars learned, the odds of success were only slightly better than those of picking a winning Powerball number. Hong studied diligently and failed repeatedly. After yet another failure, Hong experienced a breakdown and had to be carried home. He then spent weeks raving in a locked room, shouting and flailing wildly, apparently fighting demons. After a miraculous recovery, Hong described his travels up into a sacred heavenly realm where his internal organs had been replaced, and he was brought before the throne of an imposing emperor with a long golden beard.[11] The emperor called Hong his son and told him his mission was to go back to earth to chastise idolaters and destroy demons. Friends noted that Hong's personality was transformed by his experience; he was newly forceful, articulate, self-confident, and persuasive.

Several years later, Hong read a series of pamphlets distributed by evangelical Christian missionaries that gave him the key to understanding his visions. Unfortunately, the pamphlets focused primarily on the stern laws and punishments of the Hebrew Bible, with scant mention of forgiveness, redemption, or grace. It became clear to Hong that the man in the sky was the God of the Bible, the demons he was told to fight were the Manchus, and he was the Son of God. The seeds of the rebellion had been planted.

Within several years, the Taiping movement had grown from a few small congregations to a celibate army of nearly a million believers, both male and female. The Qing forces were terrified of the Taiping troops, who charged into battle with their long hair flowing free, calling them *chang mao gui* 長毛鬼, or "long-furred demons." Unlike the civilized

Chinese with hair, the Taipings were animals or demons with fur. Had the Taipings grown out their hair but bound it properly, in accord with pre-Qing Chinese tradition, they might have aroused less animosity and fear. They would have been longhaired rebels and traitors, but not demons with fur. It appears that the Taiping leaders knew exactly what they were communicating with their wild hair, and from a military perspective, it was effective.

By 1854, the Taiping armies were poised to take Beijing and gain control of the entire Chinese realm. Had they proceeded skillfully, we would be living in a very different world. Perhaps fortunately—for all but the Taiping rebels, anyway—they made a series of bad calls and ended up besieged within the massive walls of Nanjing, hanging on with ever diminishing resources until 1864, when their collapsing empire was finally destroyed. Although the Qing attempted to annihilate all traces of the movement, roaming bandit bands of long-furred demons terrorized remote districts on the periphery of China for decades.

## Covering

In the modern world, most people assume that veiling and the covering of women's hair is an Islamic custom. It is, of course, but the covering of women long predates the creation of Islam in the 600s. As Paul wrote in First Corinthians (ca. 53-57) 11:6, "In fact, a woman who will not wear a veil ought to have her hair cut off."[12] It appears that this injunction (and threat) applied only to prayer times, but the veiling of women, especially upper-class women, goes far back into antiquity. In many cultures, veiling was protective, showing that a woman was both highly moral and well placed in society. It was smart strategy for lower-class women to adopt the covering of the elite, so it soon became normative. Women who were not covered were then assumed to be immoral and suffered the consequences of that perception.[13]

In the West nuns have largely abandoned wearing the wimple, colloquially and imprecisely known as the habit. (Habit is a generic term for clerical garb, male and female.) As unflattering as it seems to moderns, it was once the basic covering of most married upper class and socially ambitious women in Europe. A trip through a good art museum will make this clear, as will a visit to the Greek islands, where older Christian women still wear traditional hair coverings. The differences between the wimple and the Iranian or Indonesian hijab are trivial; all succeed admirably in disguising the beauty of the wearer, which is precisely their point.

In the early twentieth century, modernizing autocrats like Mustafa Kemal Attaturk (1881–1938) in Turkey and Shah Mohammad Reza of Iran (1919–80) outlawed veiling and headscarves as part of the process of rapidly modernizing their societies. Many women reportedly felt naked going out in public with their hair exposed; it was deeply traumatizing for them. Religious conservatives were outraged by the state-enforced immoral, even obscene, public display of uncovered women, but they bided their time. Both countries are now deep into their respective periods of inevitable religious backlash.

In the 1990s I witnessed two small student protests in Ankara, Turkey, at METU, perhaps the most prestigious university in the Middle East. At this time Turkey was still officially a secular nation. In the first instance, leftist students protesting the forces of globalization picketed the campus McDonalds, waving signs and shouting slogans. It seemed harmless enough—the police quickly arrived, using teargas to drive the students away; the other protest, quiet and peaceful, was led by female Muslim conservatives who were violating the national ban on hijab in educational institutions by wearing headscarves. The police teargassed them, of course, but went further, viciously beating the unresisting women as they dragged them into custody. The disparity in the treatment of the protesters was jarring. It appeared that the police were far more aggrieved by quiet women wearing headscarves than by shouting leftists. The tables have since turned, and I would expect a reversal in police response were the two same protests to take place today.

# Coloring

Formulas for hair dyeing were invented roughly 6,000 years ago, which means the recipes were devised several thousand years after those for making beer, but they still appeared surprisingly early in human civilization. Our ancestors had priorities. In most instances, hair dyeing has few important religious connotations, though certain colors—blond and red especially—are associated in the popular imagination with sexual immorality. While many religions have condemned hair coloring as vain and frivolous, so far as I know, Islam is the only major religion to have debated the pros and cons of dyeing and found the practice to be religiously meritorious.

First let's look at blonds. In the heyday of the Roman Empire (ca. 30 BCE–470 CE), nearly all citizens had naturally dark hair. Romans with graying hair went to great lengths to make it appear darker, using dyes made from ashes, walnut shells, carbonized eggs, worms, leeches, and more. Some of the ingredients were probably inactive.

Graying members of both sexes also commonly used lead combs, as the accumulated lead residue darkened the hair, though at the same time it probably had adverse effects on the little gray cells just a few inches below. Respectable women covered their hair in public, and Pagan priests covered their hair when serving their gods.

Light hair was exotic and seen mostly on the slaves captured in the wars on the northern borders and on prostitutes, who wore their hair uncovered and loose. By law prostitutes were required either to bleach their hair or wear blond wigs. Over time, as greater numbers of northern European slaves were brought south, blond hair started to become more fashionable. Wigs made from blond slave hair became the rage. The custodians of morality complained bitterly, but hooker chic caught on in Rome, much as it has in Western culture today.

Eventually even respectable matrons were daring to show blond hair, either their own or a wig. (Many of the bleaching agents used to create blond hair were incredibly damaging with repeated use, so fashionable women eventually began wearing wigs of necessity, having lost much of their natural hair.) Blond hair has stayed in fashion ever since. It is now idealized, romanticized, fetishized, and practically worshiped in Western culture.

It seems likely that the link between blond hair and sexual immorality, which is in no way obvious or intuitive, started with the prostitutes of Rome. After Rome fell, the association may have survived in medieval Britain, where prostitutes revealed their availability by wearing bright yellow hoods. This seems like a logical evolution of the blond hooker motif in a culture with little expertise in dyeing hair and a fair number of natural blonds who presumably resented being mistaken for professionals. The yellow hoods seem like a good, unambiguous compromise. It appears likely, if inherently unprovable, that a dim memory of the link between blond hair and prostitution somehow made its way to the present, though in sanitized form. Nowadays blonds may, in fact, have more fun, but if they do, it is not necessarily on a commercial basis.

Strangely, precontact Samoans seem to have been huge fans of blond streaks, using lime and the tropical sun to turn parts of their elaborate and extremely creative hair styles a bleached-out yellow.[14] It must have been striking. Anthropologists have struggled to reconstruct the lives of Samoans before the arrival of Europeans, and as Margaret Mead discovered, it is a tricky business, especially where sexual practices are concerned. It turns out that Samoans, like other "primitive" peoples, enjoy misleading nosy Western interrogators. What we do know, however, is that Samoans had a lot of free time, much of which was devoted to coloring, cutting, and styling their hair. Early chroniclers were astonished by the creativity and profusion of hairstyles they encountered.[15]

Red hair is another matter entirely. First off, it is relatively rare and found primarily in Northern Europe, especially in Scotland and Ireland, though due to genetic mutations individuals with red or blond hair appear as far away as Melanesia, and dark hair can turn a reddish hue in toddlers with Kwashiorkor, a dangerous protein deficiency disease. At most 4 percent of the world's population has naturally red hair. Outside Europe red hair is rare enough to merit curiosity or raise alarm.

There is a widespread human assumption that hair color indicates temperament. Consequently redheads are often viewed as fiery, volatile, passionate, and capricious. Marion Roach, the red-haired author of *The Roots of Desire: The Myth, Meaning, and Sexual Power of Red Hair*, claims that many men believe red-haired women are sexually aggressive and insatiable, which may be the nicest traits ever attributed to redheads.[16] The supporting evidence is purely anecdotal. Red-haired men do not share in this stereotype.

In general, though, red hair fares poorly throughout human history. Red wigs were worn in Roman comedies as a kind of theatrical shorthand to inform audiences that the actor was playing a slave; Shylock, Shakespeare's moneylending caricature of a Jew, was traditionally played by an actor wearing a red wig. Medieval Christians believed that Judas had red hair as well.[17] And we haven't even gotten to witches! When it comes to popular perceptions, redheads have taken a beating throughout history, even those who aren't stepchildren. In the United States, the creepiest clowns wear vivid orange or red wigs. Oddly, it is claimed that some people find this amusing, though every person I've surveyed thinks red-haired clowns are terrifying.

One of the more positively depicted redheads in world history is the Egyptian god Set. He was an evil god, of course—the red hair gives it away—murdering his much loved brother, the god Osiris, in cold blood, but at least he was divine. Unfortunately for red-haired humans (and cattle), Osiris's worshipers would purportedly sacrifice any redheads they found, based on a somewhat convoluted theory of revenge: Set has red hair, so obviously redheaded humans (and red cows) are his devotees. You can't kill Set—he's a god, after all—but you can get back at him by sacrificing his worshipers.[18] Though redheaded humans were presumably few and far between in Egypt, Irish adventurers who happened to wander by could find themselves in big trouble. (Cattle, red or otherwise, fare poorly in all the world's religions, outside of India.) Perhaps due to Set, red was viewed as the color of evil in Egypt.

In the thirteenth century BCE, Seti I and his son Ramses II, of pharaonic and condom fame, were both apparently redheads. Naturally they worshiped Set. During their reigns, they promoted a revival of his cult, though after the death of Ramses II, Set reassumed his role as a demonic force.

The sacrifice of redheads appears to have been widespread in the ancient world; in England as late as the sixteenth century it was apparently common knowledge that you needed the fat of a redheaded man to make top-notch poison.[19] How this fat was to be obtained is unclear, but it was almost certain to be unpleasant for the red-haired man.

In the early centuries after Muhammad's death there were great debates in Islam on dyeing graying hair and beards. Scholarly observers have noted that huge, nearly inexplicable amounts of intellectual capital were expended on this issue.[20] It is not what you would expect to be an urgent concern for a millennial religion in the midst of world conquest. Curiously, the dye most commentators believe Muhammad endorsed turns hair . . . red.

A few early Muslim scholars claimed that Muhammad recommended black dye. An infamous Syrian hadith transmitter named Zuhri championed this position, because he mistakenly believed that the Torah did not permit Jews to dye their hair black. He thought it was obvious that the Prophet, the most perfect of men, would distinguish himself from Jews in every way, including the color of his hair and beard. Muslim critics pointed out that Zuhri (somewhat disreputably) dyed his own beard black, so his objectivity was questionable, and his position ultimately did not prevail.[21]

After Muslim scholars had invested many thousands of man-hours in their historical research, the majority agreed that the prophet rejected black dye for men, but accepted henna (*Lawsonia inermis*), which dyes hair and beards a range of shades running from pink through orange to bright red. This position has held for the last fourteen centuries, though there are still dissenters. The modern consensus is that the use of henna is permissible and probably commendable, even if many scholars are still not convinced that Muhammad actually dyed his own hair.

The approval of henna, as opposed to the black dyes that were also available at this time, is odd given that henna doesn't serve the most important traditional function of dye for men: camouflaging the user's age. An orange or red beard pretty much screams, "I'm decrepit!" Of course, an orange beard can also be a means of proclaiming the wearer's piety and religiosity, especially given the folk belief that Muhammad dyed his hair with henna. (Several early Muslims claimed to have hairs from the Prophet's beard that appeared to have been dyed.) As we've noted, it's usually admirable to look like the founder of your faith.

As it turns out, a henna-dyed beard has multiple benefits. It not only signifies religious devotion, but it supposedly improves eyesight and enhances male sexual vigor.[22] Old Muslim men can't lose.

# 5 FETISHIZING

Human hair has a remarkable mystique. Even though hair and nails are very similar in composition and appear to be equally useful for the working of sympathetic magic, as keepsakes they just don't have the same force of attraction or hold comparable sentimental value. An envelope of Mick Jagger's locks, trimmed back in the 1960s, sold at auction in 2013 for $6,000 (the money went to charity), while in 2011 a clipping of Justin Bieber's hair went for $40,000 on eBay. I doubt Mick's or Justin's toenail scraps would go for anywhere near as much, though I have no hard evidence. It appears that even modern, scientifically literate people, who certainly know better, somehow think that hair cuttings provide a link to the spirit of the person from whom the hair was taken.

Collecting and saving Muhammad's head and beard hair was important from the beginning of Islam. To this day, there are a number of Muslim holy sites that draw their fame from the hairs of Muhammad that they supposedly possess. Pilgrims travel great distances to bask in the spiritual power they believe radiates from the holy hair. Perhaps the most famous site is in Kashmir, a great distance from the areas where the Prophet lived and died. How Muhammad's hair got there is nearly as mysterious as the unknown ways pieces of the true cross traveled to the far reaches of Europe.

Even strict Muslims accept a measure of reverence for Muhammad, the most perfect of men, but for many the veneration of his hair crosses the line into idolatry. Should a group like the Islamic State overrun one of the holy sites preserving hairs from the Prophet's head or beard, we can expect to see it razed and the relics destroyed.

## Supernatural hair

The belief that a sorcerer can manipulate victims through their discarded hair cuttings or nail clippings is found around the globe, leading cultures to take elaborate precautions with material we moderns leave on the barbershop floor to be swept up and thrown out with the trash. A friend from Ghana, who was raised in a modern, educated Christian family, reports that his mom carefully collected his hair clippings whenever she took him to a barber. When he asked why, she claimed she was just following a silly old-wives' belief, simple superstition, but he noticed that she always took care that his hair was well-hidden inside the garbage, in a way that would foil discovery, and she made certain it was never burned.

Despite the exalted state of the human head in Hindu purity laws—few places on the body are more sacred and more easily defiled than the head—barbers in India are low caste. High caste Hindus will, of necessity, allow low caste barbers to touch their heads, but it is customary to drop payment on the ground for the barber to pick up, so defiling is the touch of a barber's hand. Ritual purification by hair washing is needed immediately after a haircut to restore caste. Hair clippings are carefully destroyed, because to this day in India, many villagers believe that the hair could be misused by sorcerers.[1]

The idea that the soul can be purified by washing the hair of the head is also found in African religions; the belief was carried to the New World by enslaved Africans who created Yoruba-Catholic religious traditions like Voudou and Santeria that preserve many traditional African themes and practices, including soul purification through ritual hair washing.

As already mentioned, during the Qing dynasty (1644–1911), all men in China were required to adopt the hairstyle of the Manchu conquerors, thereby signifying their submission. Only Buddhist and Taoist monks were exempt. Tampering with the style in any way was an act of treason that was punished with death. There was initially great resistance to this barbarian hairstyle, but over time men became proud and protective of their long queues. In 1768 when stories began spreading about mysterious, inexplicable queue thefts, the braids cut right off the heads of unsuspecting men without their knowledge, the public set up a hue and cry.

Soon several provinces were caught up in the hysteria. The spreading panic threatened to get out of hand. Though the actual number of missing queues turned out to be few (or perhaps zero), panic set in. The culprits were rumored to be renegade Buddhist monks, allied with beggars and assorted ne'er-do-wells, who were almost certainly engaged in sorcery, stealing souls as well as hair. Part of the problem was that Buddhist ordination masters often kept a tuft of hair cut from the queue of each monk they ordained, collected during the ceremony of head shaving, so in fact some monks likely were carrying bits of braids among their meager possessions. In a state of generalized panic, this looked like irrefutable evidence of sorcery, or at least some kind of misbehavior. Why would a shaven monk be carrying locks of hair, if not for dark magical purposes?

According to the rumors, the life force of the queue-cutting victims was stolen with their hair and magically transferred to full-sized paper cutouts of humans and horses, which would then come alive and be sent out on robbing expeditions. The descriptions of the actual processes by which this could be done evolved as the rumors spread, and the only hard information we have comes from confessions, usually forced by torture. As we now know, such information is often wildly inaccurate. Still the basic outline is clear.

The culprits started the process by blowing a stupefying powder into a victim's face, instantly rendering him helpless. Though this sounds improbable, several victims testified that they had been knocked out or incapacitated by this method. Next the thief snipped off the end of the victim's queue and recited magical incantations over it, transferring the victim's soul to the hair clipping. Later the hair would be tied to a paper doll that, animated by the force of the victim's stolen soul, would be sent out, like a flat zombie, to do the master sorcerer's evil will.[2]

The evidence of actual sorcery was sparse, as we might imagine, but the societal panic was real. The highly educated men who led China tended to be agnostic in matters of the spirit, but the masses were not. Therefore the magistrates and authorities of China prosecuted the reputed sorcerers with diligence, even as they discounted the reality of sorcery. Social order was threatened and must be preserved. If a few innocent monks and beggars had to be tortured, well, that was a small price to restore stability. As the "Satanic Panic" in the United States during the 1980s and the excesses of the current terrorism scares demonstrate, modern people are still susceptible to episodes of mass hysteria. Like the panicked peasants during the queue scare, we too can be calmed by a few arrests, the torture of suspects, and semi-magical bureaucratic rituals. ("Remove your shoes and laptops and place them in separate tubs. Take off your belt, and make sure you empty everything from your pockets.") Fortunately for the Chinese, the queue scare only lasted for a few months.

American Indians also believe that the soul is, or can be, held within locks of hair.

Once in North Dakota, I participated in a sweat lodge ceremony led by a respected Lakota pipe holder (spiritual leader), during which I heard several miraculous tales, one involving hair. The sweat lodge was a great deal hotter than I expected, so the finer details of the stories are a bit hazy.

Before we began, the leader told us the cautionary tale of a "bad person" at one recent ceremony who had harbored evil thoughts during the sweat. In the middle of that ceremony, while the sweat lodge was tightly closed, this bad person had mysteriously vanished into thin air, later to be found dazed and disoriented in a small town many miles away, still sweating, wearing only boxer shorts.

An hour into our ceremony, when the heat reached its greatest intensity, I remember shivering convulsively, my pulse pounding like an internal piston against the inside of my skull. I desperately tried to think of something especially wicked in the hope that I too might be teleported to the streets of Devil's Lake. Though I dimly realized it might be awkward to be found stumbling down Main Street in my underwear, at that moment it seemed like my best chance for survival. Unfortunately, I was unable to think of anything at all.

Miracles rarely happen on demand.

At some point, the spiritual leader recounted how he had recently released the soul of a young Indian girl who had died as a toddler a few years earlier. Before she was buried, her braided hair had been cut off and carefully saved. On the anniversary of her death, a group had brought her braids into the lodge, where they held a sweat in her honor. At the climax of the ceremony, the spiritual leader released the girl's soul. The mourners all claimed to hear her high-pitched cries fading in the distance, as her spirit spiraled up through the night sky into the Milky Way. We were told that the girl's soul had been held in her braids, and they were necessary to release her from this world. I never discovered how the process worked.

The belief in the power of hair to trap souls and their various energies is found in Europe and North America as well, though we don't seem especially conscious of it. We can look at a few amusing examples. My favorite is the custom of eighteenth-century British lovers to give each other clippings of their pubic hair. Some rakes even wore clippings of their paramour's pubic hair in their hatbands. (I assume they only honored a single lover at a time in this manner; sporting multiple tufts on one hat might appear ostentatious, or vulgar.) Pubic hair was enthusiastically preserved in all sorts of settings in the Georgian era. According to Tony Perrottet, the archives of the museum at St. Andrews still hold a locket containing curls of pubic hair from "the Mons Veneris of a Royal Courtesan of King George IV."[3]

Unfortunately, the magical wig woven from the apparently copious pubic hair of Charles II's mistress has gone missing. In its heyday, the wig was believed to transmit libidinal energy to its wearer, so aristocrats vied for the opportunity to enjoy its talismanic power. When last seen, the wig was reportedly thinning, perhaps from overuse, and volunteers were patching the bald spots with hair from their own lovers' pubes. You don't hear as much about pubic hair in the following Victorian period.

Victorians adored mementos made from loved ones' head hair, however. Hair jewelry was prized as a keepsake, especially when the hair came from a deceased or far-off loved one, but people also wore commercial jewelry made from anonymously sourced hair. This seems a bit creepy to me, but it's nowhere near as creepy as the effigy dolls parents commissioned when their children died. With waxen faces and weighted bodies, these lifelike (or maybe deathlike) dolls were displayed in funeral parlors and taken home as mementos. What makes the dolls especially eerie is that their heads were covered with real hair cut from the dead children. So while the bald little corpses moldered in their graves, life-sized effigy dolls reclined in the dead children's former bedrooms, wearing their best clothes and their perfectly styled hair. The faces of the surviving dolls look haunting nowadays. Many still have beautiful hair.

Perhaps the oddest thing about Victorian mourning hair is the fact that nearly everyone connected to those dead persons is now dead as well. Hair mementos that once meant a great deal to living people are now passed on as curiosities. The memorialized people, as well as those who mourned and remembered them, have long turned to dust. Their dead hair lives on.

The United States, a beacon for religious zealots and businessmen, has long been noted for its religious creativity and entrepreneurial energy. Both are on fine display in the Church of Jesus Christ of Latter-day Saints (commonly called Mormons after their revealed text, The Book of Mormon.)

In 1830, with the publication of The Book of Mormon, Euro-Americans were finally given a definitive, biblically grounded explanation for the origin of the American Indians—they're remnants of the lost tribes of Israel. The explanation was long overdue.

In 1844, Joseph Smith, the visionary founder of the Mormon religion, and his brother Hyrum were dragged from jail by a mob and murdered. Followers wasted no time seeking sanctified relics of their martyred prophet and his brother. Walking canes were fashioned from the wood of the temporary coffins in which the two brothers had lain in state. The most prized of these "canes of martyrdom" are those with tiny braids, woven from the brothers' hair, on display in their handles under glass disks cut from the coffin covers. In 1857, Heber Kimball, one of the "twelve apostles" of the early Church, gave a sermon in which he praised the spiritual power of the canes:

> I want to carefully preserve my cane, and when I am done with it here, I shall hand it down to my heir, with instructions to him to do the same. And the day will come when there will be multitudes who will be healed and blessed through the instrumentality of those canes, and the devil cannot overcome those who have them.[4]

While Mr. Kimball does not specify exactly how the canes work or detail the source of their supernatural power, I am willing to bet it's the hair that works the magic.

# 6 CONCLUSIONS

As promised, we will not propose a universal theory of hair. It's clear from this quick tour of global hair customs that no one set of explanations can possibly be adequate. There are, however, a few general principles to consider.

Human hair rules can be compared to languages, in that each option—shaving, trimming, styling, covering, dyeing—functions like a phoneme. Though different languages favor different phonemes and combine them in distinctive ways to form words and sentences that convey meaning, the actual number of sound units used in human languages is reasonably small. The number of hair manipulations is similarly limited. There are only so many things you can do with your hair, and if you can think of something, someone, somewhere, has already done it. However, its meaning, then and there, might not be what you expect, here and now.

A very few phonemes have nearly universal meaning. For example, "ma" means mother in a great number of languages. This is presumably because ma (or mama) is often the first sound babies produce. ("She just said my name!") Analogous reasoning explains why "da" or "ba" (dada, baba) often means father, across unrelated language groups.

Similarly, the most stark hair options—shaving/control and untrammeled growth/wildness—*tend* to have universal meanings. The covering of women's hair also means roughly the same thing worldwide. An explorer entering a newly discovered land where adult women wear full head coverings would certainly know, without being told, that the women were not available. Yet even these basic "phonemes" may display wide variance in meaning. A shaven head indicates disgrace or shame when used as a punishment, yet a similar hairless head might signify controlled rage on a White supremacist, self-confident power on a CEO, dedication to a life of celibacy on a Buddhist monk, a recent life transition on a Hindu, and mourning on a Lakota. It's complex.

Even within one culture, a particular style might embrace opposing meanings. We see this with words, as well, as they constantly morph in import. I remember trying to explain to a Chinese exchange student how "bad" can mean both horrible and really cool. It all depends on the context, I explained, to the total frustration of the student. The same is true of hairstyles, and it's incredibly hard to judge context in unfamiliar settings.

Even within our own small communities, we often cannot understand the verbal slang and subtle hair conventions of local subgroups. Just listen to the older generations grumble about the kids, their language, and their hair! The young know exactly what they are saying with their slang and hair, even though the nuance is lost on the rest of us. That's just the point, of course. How much greater are the challenges when encountering religions and cultures far different from our own! When we get into the more complex and subtle manipulations of hair, religious rules and cultural context are paramount.

Religions use hair to create identity and accentuate difference. From a distance, the great Middle Eastern monotheisms—Judaism, Christianity, Islam, and their numerous smaller relatives—share enormous similarities, much as the many forms of Hinduism, Buddhism, and Jainism appear generically related in beliefs and practices. The differences that seem so great to the true believers of each faith are objectively dwarfed by the remarkable overlaps and similarities. Distinctive dress and hair rules then become essential aspects of the process of differentiation, separation, and claims to unique status. Once God or the divine is invoked, rules tend to become absolute and rigid. This gives them extraordinary longevity. The meaning of hairstyles can change far more rapidly in secularized societies than deeply religious ones, or so it appears.

For all our cleverness as symbol-using primates, we tend to make a great number of errors, or mistranslations, when reading others' hair. When at home, we tend to assume all members of our culture share our personal understandings of hair symbolism. When abroad we often suppose that people in other lands share our home society's consensual assumptions.

Now when it comes to different languages, everyone knows translation is necessary, yet we assume somatic symbolism is universal. It isn't. (As US troops in Iraq discovered to their dismay, a raised hand does not mean "stop" in the Middle East.) We can safely assume that the subtle meanings of the various beards, turbans, head coverings, haircuts, and moustaches we encounter are almost certainly not quite what we think.

For an inert, dead substance poking out of follicles all over our bodies, hair has certainly generated its fair share of passion, attention, care, revulsion, anger, attraction, and affront. It's undeniable that hair holds real, tangible power—at least in the world of interpersonal relationships, if not in a spiritual or supernatural realm.

Over the course of a lifetime, the average human spends far more time messing with her or his hair—cutting, combing, brushing, shaving, plucking, dyeing, washing, styling—than in nearly any other leisure activity. And we can't do it all by ourselves; most of us need help. Forget prostitution—I'm pretty sure hairstyling is the world's oldest profession.

The meaning of hair—yours and others'—varies with each observer, depending on each individual's idiosyncratic blend of personal, cultural, ethnic, gender, and religious identities—and also, of course, their political, musical, artistic, fashion, and sexual tastes. For all its obviousness, its ordinariness, and its universality, hair is still mysterious, possessing an uncanny ability to attract, shock, surprise, offend, and confound. You would think humans would have hair completely figured out by now—after all, we've been styling it since our ancient hominid ancestors first discovered mud, fat, sticks, feathers, and sharp rocks—yet somehow it slips through our grasp.

It's remarkable and humbling to realize that, in the final analysis, the only certain thing we know about hair is that, however it is styled and whatever shape it takes, it always means *something* to every person who sees it, though few of us may agree on what that something is.

# NOTES

## Chapter 1

**1** Claude Vorilhon [Raël], *Le livre qui dit la vérité. J'ai rencontré un extra terrestre* (*The Book Which Tells the Truth: I Have Encountered an Extra-terrestrial*) (Clermont-Ferrand: L'Edition du Message, 1974), 58–59.

**2** As posed by the Barbarians in their sardonic 1966 radio hit.

**3** 1 Corinthians 11:14–15.

**4** Jason Horowitz, "Mitt Romney's prep school classmates recall pranks, but also troubling incidents," *The Washington Post*, May 11, 2012.

**5** See www.nytimes.com/slideshow/2012/09/12/us/politics/1?stanford-4.html.

## Chapter 2

**1** Edwin B. Liem, M.D., et al., "Anesthetic Requirement Is Increased in Redheads," *Anesthesiology* 101, no. 2 (August 2004): 279–83, www.ncbi.nlm.nih.gov/pmc/articles/PMC1362956/.

2   Christopher Siriano, *Images of America: The House of David* (Charleston, SC: Arcadia Publishing, 2007), 17.

3   Christian Bromberger, "Hair: From the West to the Middle East through the Mediterranean," *The Journal of American Folklore* 121, no. 482 (Fall 2008): 381.

4   Sue Walsh, "Bikini Fur and Fur Bikinis," in *The Last Taboo: Women and Body Hair*, ed. Karin Lesnik-Oberstein (Manchester, UK: Manchester University Press), 166.

5   Quoted in Eric Reinders, *Borrowed Gods and Foreign Bodies: Christian Missionaries Imagine Chinese Religion* (Los Angeles: University of California Press, 2004), 184.

6   Reinders, *Borrowed Gods*, 184–86.

# Chapter 3

1   Mohamed Atta, "Last words of a terrorist," *The Guardian*, September 30, 2001, www.theguardian.com/world/2001/sep/30/terrorism.september113.

2   Sahih Al-Bukhari, *Hadith*, Volume 8, Book 74, Number 312, www.sahih-bukhari.com/Pages/Bukhari_8_74.php. The Hadith are reports from the early Muslim community detailing the words or actions of the Prophet and his closest companions. Muslim scholars have invested a great deal of effort in determining the reliability of these stories and have developed an impressive rating system. This Hadith is considered to be sound.

3   Wynne Parry, "Live Science," November 7, 2013, www.livescience.com/41028-lice-reveal-clues-to-human-evolution.html.

4   See www.claireaccuhair.com/.

5   BBC, September 24, 2001, www.bbc.co.uk/worldservice/
    people/highlights/010622_hair.shtml.

6   "Venezuela's Maduro pledges action on women's hair
    thieves," August 15, 2013, www.bbc.com/news/world-latin-
    america-23707452.

7   Bromberger, "Hair," 381.

8   Fatema Soudavar Farmanfarmaian, "'Haft Qalam Ārāyish':
    Cosmetics in the Iranian World," *Iranian Studies* 33, no. 3/4
    (Summer–Autumn 2000): 309.

9   Jill Burke's blog, "Did Renaissance Women Remove Their
    Body Hair?" December 9, 2012, https://renresearch.wordpress.
    com/2012/12/09/did-renaissance-women-remove-their-body-
    hair/.

10  Farmanfarmaian, "Cosmetics," 310.

11  E. R. Leach, "Magical Hair," *The Journal of the Royal
    Anthropological Institute of Great Britain and Ireland* 88, no. 2
    (1958): 147–64.

12  Buddhaghosa, *Visudhimagga: The Path of Purification*,
    trans. Bhikkhu Nanamoli (Kandy, Sri Lanka: The Buddhist
    Publication Society), 244, http://www.accesstoinsight.org/lib/
    authors/nanamoli/PathofPurification2011.pdf.

10  Buddhaghosa, *Path*, 45.

14  See Gananath Obeyesekere, *Medusa's Hair: An Essay on
    Personal Symbols and Religious Experience* (Chicago:
    University of Chicago Press, 1981), 38–40. This monograph
    is a landmark in the study of ascetic hair and has not been
    supplanted by more recent work.

15  "Ban on Prison Beards Violates Muslim Rights, Supreme
    Court Says," *New York Times*, January 20, 2015, www.nytimes.
    com/2015/01/21/us/prison-beard-ban-gregory-holt-ruling.html.

16  "Rasta inmates spend decade in isolation for dreadlocked hair,"
    *USA Today*, May 8, 2010, http://usatoday30.usatoday.com/
    news/religion/2010-05-08-rastafarian-dreadlocks_N.htm.

17  Heaven's Gate: www.heavensgate.com/.

# Chapter 4

1  I am following the lead of my American Indian students at the
   University of North Dakota. They struggled to convince me
   that they did not wish to be called "Native Americans." As far
   as they were concerned, that was neocolonial white persons'
   political correctness. They were American Indians. It took
   years of practice, but I finally got it.

2  Margaret Holmes Williamson, "Powhatan Hair," *Man*, Royal
   Anthropological Institute of Great Britain and Ireland New
   Series 14, no. 3 (1979): 392–413.

3  To get a sense of Eliot's priorities see *The Eliot Tracts: With
   Letters from John Eliot to Thomas Thorowgood and Richard
   Baxter*, ed. Michael P. Clark (Westport, CT: Greenwood
   Publishing Group, 2003).

4  "Human hair thefts strike US salons," BBC, June 3, 2011,
   www.bbc.com/news/world-us-canada-13632447.

5  Stacy Patton, "Rachel Dolezal Case Leaves a Campus
   Bewildered and Some Scholars Disgusted," *The Chronicle of
   Higher Education*, June 17, 2015, http://chronicle.com/article/
   Rachel-Dolezal-Case-Leavesa/230947/?cid=at&utm_source
   =at&utm_medium=en.

6  For an engaging insider history, see Douglas R. A. Mack,
   *From Babylon to Rastafari: Origin and History of the Rastafari*

*Movement* (Chicago: Research Associates School Times Publications, 1999).

**7** Mack, *Rastafari*, 51.

**8** Richard C. Salter, "Sources and Chronology in Rastafari Origins," *Nova Religio: The Journal of Alternative and Emergent Religions* 9, no. 1 (August 2005): 5–31.

**9** See Edward E. Curtis IV, "Science and Technology in Elijah Muhammad's Nation of Islam: Astrophysical Disaster, Genetic Engineering, UFOs, White Apocalypse, and Black Resurrection," *Nova Religio* 20, no. 1 (August 2016).

**10** Edmundo Lupieri, *The Mandaeans: The Last Gnostics*, trans. Charles Hindley (Grand Rapids, MI: Wm. B. Eerdmans, 2001), 7.

**11** This sounds a great deal like a traditional spontaneous shamanic initiation of the sort reported in anthropological literature and discussed in Mircea Eliade's *Shamanism: Archaic Techniques of Ecstasy*; in its broad structure, it also sounds a bit like a modern alien abduction account.

**12** This is the wording from the Jerusalem Bible. Some scholars maintain that this passage was inserted into Corinthians by a later author, so it is not in fact the opinion of Paul. While this may be true, it scarcely matters, because the words have been believed to be Paul's from the earliest days of the church.

**13** For a breezy, but accurate, introduction to the history of women's covering, see Max Dashu, "Some Thoughts on the Veil," www.suppressedhistories.net/articles/veil.html.

**14** Jeanette Marie Mageo, "Hairdos and Don'ts: Hair Symbolism and Sexual History in Samoa," *Man*, New Series 29, no. 2 (1994): 408.

**15** Mageo, "Hairdos," 407–08.

**16** Marion Roach, *The Roots of Desire: The Myth, Meaning, and Sexual Power of Red Hair* (New York: Bloomsbury, 2005), 27–28.

**17** Roach, *Roots*, 37–41.

**18** Ibid., 49.

**19** Ibid., 10.

**20** G. H. A. Juynboll, "Dyeing the Hair and Beard in Early Islam: A Hadith-analytical Study," *Arabica*, T. 33, Fasc. 1 (March 1986): 49–75.

**21** Juynboll, "Dyeing the Hair and Beard in Early Islam," 49–75.

**22** Farmanfarmaian, "Cosmetics," 313.

# Chapter 5

**1** Sir James Frazier has compiled a number of beliefs about hair sorcery, among many other oddities, in *The Golden Bough*, his classic text of armchair anthropology. The section on the disposal of hair and nails is available online at: http://www.bartleby.com/196/51.html.

**2** For a book-length treatment of this fascinating story, see Phillip A. Kuhn, *Soulstealers: The Chinese Sorcery Scare of 1768* (Cambridge, MA.: Harvard University Press, 1990).

**3** Tony Perrottet, "Hellfire Holidays" *Slate*, December 18, 2009, www.slate.com/articles/life/welltraveled/features/2009/hellfire_holidays/gentlemen_charge_your_indecent_props.html.

**4** "Joseph Smith Jr: The Coffin Canes, The Joseph Smith and Emma Hale Smith Historical Society Web page, December 9, 2013, www.josephsmithjr.org/index.php/history/joseph-smith-jr/201-the-coffin-canes.

# INDEX

9/11 *see* September 11, 2001
1904 World's Fair    33

Abraham    40
Absalom    3–4
Adi Granth    92
Adi Shankara    56
Advaita Vedanta    56
Afghanistan    47
Africa    23–4, 80, 113
African Americans    46, 76–9,
        84–6
Ainu    20–1
Allah    39–40, 49, 84
American Civil War    27
American Indians    36, 70–5,
        115–17, 119, 122
Amish    60–2, 76
Ankara, Turkey    104
Ann Arbor (MI)    8
anorexia    21
antiwar movement    6, 9
Applewhite, Marshall
        Herff    66–7

asceticism    2, 52–60, 63
        *see also* celibacy
Asia    24, 36–7, 44, 63, 81, 93
        *see also* China; India;
        Japan
Atta, Mohamed    39
Attaturk, Mustafa Kemal    103

Babylon    41
baseball    31–2
beards *see* facial hair
Beats    6
Benton Harbor (MI)    27, 30
Bergholz (OH)    60–2
Bible    2–4, 13, 29, 30, 61, 70,
        74, 80, 81, 90, 101, 102–3
Bieber, Justin    111
Black Star Line    80
body hair    20, 22, 25, 35, 41,
        42–3, 48, 49 *see also*
        pubic hair
Book of Mormon    118, 119
Brahmins    86, 87, 89
braids *see* dreadlocks; queues

Bromberg, Christian   47
Buddha   90
Buddhaghosa   53
    *The Path of Purification*
        53–4
Buddhism   7, 11, 40, 52–5, 57,
        90, 113, 114, 122, 123
Byzantine Empire   64–5

Calvinists *see* Puritans
castration   52, 64, 66, 67
celibacy   28, 52, 56, 57, 60, 66,
        72, 87, 122
Celts   64
Cerularius   65
Charles I, King of England   13
Charles II, King of
        England   117
China   8–9, 35, 37, 45, 54–5,
        83, 97–102, 113–15
Christian Israelites   28
Christianity   7, 13, 28, 40–1,
        63–5, 73–4, 75, 76,
        80, 97, 100, 101, 103,
        108, 123
*Chronicle of Higher
        Education*   78
Church of Jesus Christ of
        Latter-day Saints *see*
        Mormons
circumcision   40, 94, 97
Claire Accuhair   44
Confucianism   98–9

Confucius   98
control   51, 60–2, 69–70, 74,
        75–6, 122
counterculture *see* antiwar
        movement; Beats;
        hippies; punks
Cranbrook School   9
Cro-Magnons   33

David, King of Israel   3–4
depilation   4, 15–16, 17, 20,
        33, 39–40, 42–3, 46–7,
        48–51, 52–6, 57, 58–60,
        69, 77, 95
Detroit (MI)   84
Dhammananda
        Bhikkhuni   52–3
DNA   23–4
dogs   19
Dolezal, Rachel   78–9
Dominica   81–2
Dread Act of 1974
        (Dominica)   81
dreadlocks   56–7, 63, 79, 81–3
dress codes   10
Druids   64
Duke University   5
dyeing *see* hair coloring

effigy dolls   118
Egypt   42–3, 48, 49, 108–9
Eliot, John   73–5
End Times   28, 33–4

England   109
English Civil War   74
Enkidu   42
*Epic of Gilgamesh*   41–2
Ethiopia   80, 82, 84
Europe   24–5, 103, 105, 107,
          112, 117
Executive Order 44
          (Missouri)   82

facial hair   33–4, 35, 36–7, 39,
          40–1, 42, 43, 46, 47, 51, 61,
          62, 63, 65, 72, 81, 87, 89,
          93, 94, 95–6, 109, 110, 124
Fard, W. D.   84
Farrakhan, Louis   85
fetishizing   16
filial piety   98
France   11, 69
Freud, Sigmund   35, 47
fur   18, 25, 26, 34–6, 42, 101–2

Garvey, Marcus   79–80, 86
gender identification   6, 8, 11,
          27, 30–2, 33–4, 52–3, 54,
          66, 71–2, 87, 95, 124
George IV, King of
          England   117
Gilgamesh   *see Epic of
          Gilgamesh*
*Good Hair* (Rock)   77
Gowing, T. S.   36
Great Depression   5

Great Peace *see* Taiping
          movement
Greece   42, 103
grooming *see* hairstyling
Guru Nanak *see* Nanak

habits *see* wimples
Haile Selassie I, Emperor of
          Ethiopia   80, 82, 84
hair coloring   104–10
hair colors *see* hair typologies
hair covering   11–12, 13, 44,
          76, 83, 85, 93, 96, 97, 98,
          102–4, 105, 106, 122, 124
hair cutting *see* hairstyling
hair jewelry   118, 119
hair removal *see* depilation;
          head shaving
hair straightening   77
hairstyling
          cultural significance   2, 3–4,
                    6, 7, 8, 9–10, 11, 14–15,
                    16, 20–1, 27, 30–1, 34–5,
                    36, 50–1, 70–1, 76–7,
                    78–9, 81, 82–3, 85–6,
                    87–8, 89, 100, 102–4, 105,
                    107–10, 113–15, 121–5
          social significance   1–6, 7,
                    8, 9–10, 11–13, 14, 17, 18,
                    20, 22, 27–33, 36, 51–2,
                    70, 72, 73, 75–6, 77, 78–9,
                    85–6, 87–8, 89, 93, 97–8,
                    101–2, 107–8, 123, 125

hair typologies   22–5
Hamam   48
Hare Krishnas *see* International
      Society for Krishna
      Consciousness (ISKCON)
Harvey, Douglas   8
head shaving   8–9, 11, 44,
      45–6, 51, 52–6, 58–9, 60,
      63–5, 66, 67, 69, 71, 72,
      114, 122
Heaven's Gate   66–7
henna   110
Herodotus   42
Hinduism   46, 49, 55,
      56–7, 86–91, 92, 94, 96,
      112–13, 122, 123
hippies   6–7, 8, 10
Hong Xiuquan   100–1
House of David   27–33
Humbert, Cardinal   65
humiliation *see* shaming
Hutchinson, Anne   73
hygiene   39–40, 43, 49, 83,
      86, 93

identity   1–2, 15, 51–60,
      78–83, 86–102, 123
      *see also* African
      Americans; American
      Indians; hairstyling;
      individual religions
India   45–6, 55–6, 57–8, 77,
      86–96, 113

International Society for
      Krishna Consciousness
      (ISKCON)   89–90
Iran   50, 95, 103
Iraq   124
ISIS *see* Islamic State (ISIS)
Islam   7, 13, 33–4, 39–40, 46–8,
      49, 61, 62–3, 76, 77, 84,
      85, 91, 92, 94, 96–7,
      102–4, 105, 109–10,
      111–12, 123
Islamic State (ISIS)   112
Israelites   4

Jagger, Mick   111
Jah *see* Haile Selassie I,
      Emperor of Ethiopia
Jainism   57–8, 90, 123
Jamaica   79–81, 82
Jamestown Colony   71–2
Japan   20–1, 35
Jesus   7, 8, 84
John the Baptist   97
Jones, Martha   78
Judaism   7, 13, 40–1, 44, 45,
      46, 82, 87, 94, 97, 108,
      109, 110, 123

Kabilsingh, Chatsumarn
      *see* Dhammananda
      Bhikkhuni
Kaur, Harnaam   95
Kentucky Derby   76

keratin 18, 24
Key West (FL) 5, 12
khalsa 93–7
Kimball, Herbert 119
Krishna 89, 90
Kwashiorkor 107

lanugo hair 21
Leach, E. R. 51
    "Magical Hair" 51
lice 43

"Magical Hair" (Leach) 51
Mahavira 57
Manchus 98–9
Mandeans 97
manipulation see hairstyling
marital status 6, 44, 48, 87
Marley, Bob 83
Massachusetts Bay Colony 13
Mead, Margaret 107
men 1–4, 5, 6, 8, 9, 10, 13,
        19, 20, 21, 22, 27, 30–2,
        36, 46–7, 51, 52, 58–60,
        61–2, 63–4, 67, 72, 75,
        81–3, 85, 86–7, 97, 98–9,
        108, 109–10, 113–14
Mennonites 11–12, 76
Middle East 40–1, 50, 76, 97,
        123, 124
Missouri 82
monastics see asceticism;
        celibacy

Mongolia 45
Mormons 82, 118–19
mourning 42, 86, 94, 118,
        119, 122
moustaches see facial hair
Muhammad 7, 40, 84, 109,
        110, 111–12
Muhammad, Elijah 84–6
Muhammad, W. D. 85
Mullet, Samuel 60–2

NAACP see National
        Association for the
        Advancement of Colored
        People (NAACP)
Nanak 91–2
Nashville (TN) 10
National Association for the
        Advancement of Colored
        People (NAACP) 78
Nation of Islam (NOI) 79, 84–6
Native Americans see
        American Indians
Nazirites 2, 30, 81, 82
Nazis 11, 60
Neanderthals 24, 33
neoteny 19–20
NOI see Nation of Islam (NOI)
North Dakota 115–17
nudity 57–8

Oak Creek (WI) 96–7
O'Connor, Sinead 11

*Path of Purification, The*
    (Buddhaghosa) 53–4
Paul 7, 13, 26, 61, 102–3
Pentecostals 76
Perrottet, Tony 117
Philistines 3
phonemes 121–2
piercings 11
pigtails *see* queues
politics 11, 15, 65
Poole, Elijah *see* Muhammad,
    Elijah
pornography 49
power 3–4, 6, 10, 15, 31,
    36–7, 41–2, 47, 51, 56,
    57, 72, 79, 101–2, 107–8,
    109, 111–12, 115–17,
    119, 122, 124
Powhatan 71–3
"Powhatan Hair"
    (Williamson) 71–2
pubic hair 22, 26, 41, 43, 46,
    47, 48–9, 50, 60, 93, 117
punks 10
Puritans 13, 73, 74, 75
Purnell, Benjamin 28–9

Quakers 13
queues 98–9

Raël 3
Rastafari 18, 63, 79–83, 84,
    86, 97

Rastafari Makonnen *see* Haile
    Selassie I, Emperor of
    Ethiopia
razors 42–3
religion 3, 4, 7–8, 11–12,
    13–15, 18, 27–33, 39–40,
    44, 45–8, 49, 60–2, 70,
    72, 73–4, 75, 76, 79–83,
    84–97, 102–4, 108–10,
    112–13, 114, 122–3
    *see also* individual groups
Renaissance 50
renunciation *see* asceticism
Reza, Mohammad, Shah of
    Iran 103
ritual 18, 46–8, 58–9, 64–5, 113
Roach, Marion 107–8
    *The Roots of Desire: The
    Myth, Meaning, and
    Sexual Power of Red
    Hair* 107–8
Rock, Chris 77
    *Good Hair* 77
Roman Empire 105, 106, 108
Romney, Mitt 9–10
*Roots of Desire, The: The Myth,
    Meaning, and Sexual
    Power of Red Hair*
    (Roach) 107–8
Royalists 74

Samoa 106–7
Samson and Delilah 2–3

Santeria   113
scalp locks   71
scarification   55
sentimentality   2, 111, 117, 118, 119
    *see also* mourning
September 11, 2001   39
sexuality   6, 11, 15, 22, 25, 26–7, 29, 35–6, 42, 44, 48, 49, 51–6, 64–5, 66–7, 72, 76, 87, 89, 105, 106, 107–8, 110, 117, 122
Shakespeare, William   33, 108
shamans   72
shaming   8, 9, 60–2, 64, 88, 122
*shikha*   86, 89, 90
Shiva   7, 56
Sikhs   18, 39, 83, 91–7
slavery   76, 105–6, 113
Smith, Hyrum   119
Smith, Joseph   119
sorcery   112, 113, 114–15
soul   2, 18, 115–17
South America   45, 46
Southcott, Joanna   28
Spokane (WA)   78
Stanford University   9
stereotypes   25, 31, 36, 74, 107–8, 123
Sufis   91
sugaring   51 *see also* depilation
Sumeria   41
superstition   112–17, 119, 124

Taiping movement   100–2
Taliban   47, 49
Tamil Nadu   88
Taoism   113
tattoos   11, 21, 98
terminal hair *see* body hair; facial hair; pubic hair
Thailand   52–3
threading   51 *see also* depilation
Tirupati Balaji Temple   45
tonsuring *see* head shaving
Torah   44, 109
Turkey   103, 104

UFOs   3
UNIA *see* Universal Negro Improvement Association (UNIA)
Universal Negro Improvement Association (UNIA)   80
University of Michigan   78
US Navy   5
US Supreme Court   63

Vaishnavas   89
*vajibt*   50
vegetarianism   28, 30, 32
veiling   102–4
vellus hair   21, 22
Victorians   36, 117–18
Virginia   63, 71–2
virility   22, 31, 36–7, 51–2, 72

Vishnu   45, 89, 90
Vorilhon, Claude *see* Raël
Voudou   113

Washtenaw County (MI)   8
weaves   46, 77
wigs   43, 44–6, 77, 105–6
Williamson, Margaret
 Holmes   71–2
 "Powhatan Hair"   71–2
wimples   103

women   4, 13, 19, 20, 21, 22, 26,
 27, 30, 32, 33–4, 45–6, 48,
 50, 51, 52–3, 58, 59–60,
 61, 62, 64, 72, 75–6, 83,
 85, 87–8, 95, 97, 102–4,
 105, 106, 107–8, 122
World War II   5

yoga   56–7

Zuhri   109–10